SECRETS OF

SUCCESSFUL BOARDS

The Best From The
Non-Profit Pros

COMPILED AND EDITED BY

CAROL WEISMAN

SECRETS OF

SUCCESSFUL BOARDS

The Best From The
Non-Profit Pros

COMPILED AND EDITED BY
CAROL WEISMAN

Published by
F. E. Robbins & Sons Press
St. Louis, Missouri

Illustrations by Sandy Sineff

Cover and text layout by Ad Graphics, Tulsa, OK • 918-252-1103

Printed in the United States of America.

ISBN 0-9666168-1-2

Acknowledgments

The best part of doing this book has been the chance to work with the nonprofit pros. Susan Ellis and Terrie Temkin, thanks for being the first with your chapters! I love and appreciate your attention to detail and timeliness. Charlie Brown, you managed to get your work in despite changing jobs and getting married. Speaking of marriage, I'm so glad you got your chapter in so that you could walk down the aisle in peace, Kat Rosqueta. No one makes me laugh like you, David LaGreca. Even when I called to yell, plead and beg for your to finish your chapter, I got off the phone chuckling. Steve Epner, thanks for letting me M.C. the celebration of your 50th birthday and for getting your chapter done while completing your "Year 2000 Book," and running around the country speaking and consulting. Don Kramer, thanks for taking the time to meet me at the National Speaker's Convention. Your legal newsletter will no doubt keep many of my clients out of jail. Fern Koch, your continual enthusiasm for the project has been a great help. Mike Schroeder thanks for stealing some time from writing fiction to devote to this project.

To Katie Burnham and Jill Muehrcke from the Society for Nonprofit Organizations and the Learning Institute for Nonprofit Organizations, thanks for giving me friendship and encouragement as well as both print and video opportunities.

Special thanks to the staff of the National Center for Nonprofit Boards for introducing me to the "Greats of Governance" at their yearly leadership conference. Thanks to founder Nancy Axelrod, Maureen Robinson, Rick Moyers and now Judy O'Connor, I've had the opportunity to learn from Robert Lewis, Frances Hesselbein, William Bowen and Billy Shore, just to name a few. And also for letting me be a part of "Speaking of Money" and "A Corporate Employee's Guide to Nonprofit Board Service."

To my speaker's group: Sam Silverstein, Linda Nash, Tony Ruesing, Steve Epner and Karyn Buxman, thanks for letting me try out new material and fail, fix and rewrite in private.

To my heroes of the National Speaker's Association: Paul Radde, Mark LeBlanc and Joel Weldon for helping with the art of seating an audience or board, and the business and technique of speaking.

Orville Ray Wilson from the Gorilla Group, thanks for the title.

And for their unwavering support, my sister Nancy Wilking, my pal Marty London and the three men I love: Frank, Teddy and Jono Robbins. You make it all worthwhile.

Table of Contents

Introduction

I thought of writing this book myself. For about one second. What I love about sitting in a board room are the different points of view, the different voices, the different styles, which is why I decided to ask my colleagues to share their expertise, joy and insight. No attempt has been made at uniformity, other than spelling, grammar and punctuation.

The purpose of this book is to give board members some tools and advice on how to do well. This is not a book of best practices, but rather, like a board, the opinion of many different folks.

Everyone has unique talents: I have two. The most unusual is that I'm almost an idiot savant at getting upgrades on airplanes. (I do not have a coach bottom. I have a first class bottom!) The other is recruiting marvelous people to get involved in exciting projects.

We hope this book will help you share your unique talents so as to achieve the mission of a group you care about.

You never know where you'll find
that next great board member.

CHAPTER 1

Building a Board with a
Passion for Mission

Carol E. Weisman

For any nonprofit organization, finding the ideal Board of Directors is a worthy goal. And finding the ideal board – full of people who are truly passionate about the cause – is a dream come true. In most groups, a board with a passion for the mission can mean the difference between existence and extinction. That may sound drastic, but I've worked with plenty of nonprofits who don't live up to their potential because of an ineffective board.

In some cases, there's a tendency to think passion doesn't matter. If Mr. Big Bucks has accepted your board nomination, and is only passionate about writing one huge check per year, that may be enough. But most of the time, it's not.

Passion doesn't necessarily require your board members to live and breathe your cause. If they do, that's great. There's a lot to be said for having board members who walk into the room overflowing with raw enthusiasm. In my mind, a more attainable goal is getting a boardroom full of people who are passionate about sharing their gifts on behalf of your mission. In other words, whatever your board members bring to the party – whether it's connections in high places, deep pockets, or an amazing ability to tell your story to an audience – they are inspired to share their strengths.

So, where does the passion come from? Well, it starts with us, the people who participate in the board recruitment process. There are many things we can do, from the beginning, to create a committed board.

My goal in this chapter is to give you ideas on how to build a board with a passion for your mission, no matter how large or small your agency. I happen to be somewhat of an expert in this area. Not because I'm perfect (although my husband will tell you emphatically that I am), but because I've been down the road many times. I've made all the mistakes and I've seen how passion fizzles out.

I have several personal stories to share, plus examples from real life boards. I hope the lessons I've learned – as well as the lessons they've learned – will get you started in the right direction. Over time, I would like to think that a passion for mission will become a natural part of your nominating and recruiting process.

BOARD ASSESSMENT:
An Absolute Necessity

It's hard to have the foundation for a passionate board unless you know where you are and where you need to be as an organization. In part, this means determining the demographics of the people you serve. It also means taking a close look at current board members.

But first, take a step back, because you can't really address those issues until you answer one important question: What exactly is your mission?

Know thy mission, know thy direction.

Unfortunately, the nonprofit's mission rarely gets the time and attention it deserves. Why? My theory is we don't think of our groups as businesses. Granted, we aren't in business to make a profit. But we are in business to make money for the causes we support. What's more, as we grow in size or scope, sometimes our mission changes.

Here's one way to look at it. Let's say you and I both like to cook (the cooking thing is pure fantasy on my part). And let's say we decide to deliver food to a few AIDS patients who need our help.

Before you know it, we're bringing food to 300 AIDS patients. We have a commercial kitchen and a food distribution center. We've incorporated as a 501(c)(3). We're looking to hire staff. And we also have a board. Then, we find out that 10,000 people in our community who are elderly or disabled could use this service.

At this point, we really have two choices: We can grow, which is fine, but then we need a different kind of board. Or, we can just stay small, and only deliver food to our 300 people with AIDS.

I'm sharing this example to illustrate an important point: We have to realize that our mission is a living, breathing goal and it may change over time. If we don't revisit our mission, we may lose sight of our goals. And if we go into the recruiting process with blinders on, our board doesn't stand a chance.

Comfort is cheap. Cure costs.

It's okay to not have a power board if we have a smaller mission. We don't need Bill Gates to buy a new toaster. On the other hand, if our mission evolves into raising money towards finding a cure for AIDS, we're in a whole different ballpark. While we don't need the CEO of a Fortune 500 company to buy an appliance, we sure as heck can't fund a $30 million campaign without some serious clout.

Passion thrives in diversity.

Diversity is not about being socially correct. Diversity on your board simply makes sense because it's profitable.

In Ann Morrison's 1992 book, "The New Leaders," she cites 12 companies as models of diversity. Of these, 11 were included on Fortune Magazine's list of most admired companies – and three of them won the Malcolm Baldridge Award for quality. Diversity is good business. And remember, we are running a business.

Diversity is broader than race and gender. Think about it: If you have a black, white, and Hispanic person on your board, and they all came from a Fortune 100 company, grew up in middle class America, and went to an Ivy League School, you may not have as much diversity as you would think.

Diversity means different things to different boards. I was doing some work with a Catholic nonprofit. I asked them if they had a diverse board and they said, "yes, we have a German Catholic, an Italian Catholic and an Irish Catholic. And we're looking for a Mexican Catholic." And then, I asked the most outrageous question: "What about Catholic women?" What I learned from their answer is this: diversity to them was not race and gender. It was different cultural adaptations of Catholicism.

Abandon your assumptions. Never assume, for example, that one Mexican Catholic knows how all Mexican Catholics think and feel.

To help yourself kick the assumption habit, I encourage you to take this solemn pledge: "I will not expect women to serve food and clean up. I will not expect men to pick up the tab and move furniture."

I'm sure you can think of other assumptions we make based on someone's race, gender or ethnic background. For diversity to work, the assumptions have to go.

Practice the Platinum Rule. We've all heard of the golden rule. But when it comes to diversity, the Platinum Rule is more appropriate: Treat others as they would want to be treated.

My kids and I got into a big ruckus because they didn't do anything for me for Mother's Day. So I said, "look guys, you don't like surprises, you prefer cash, and you want to pick things out yourselves. And that's what you get, 'cause that's what you want. Now, I'm going to tell you what I want: I want a surprise, I want it wrapped, and I want it on the day of the occasion. And I expect presents three times a year. On my birthday, on Mother's Day, and on Christmas." And then my son said, "What about Halloween?"

Now, I'm not sure they got the point. But when you bring diversity to your board, the point is clear: the trick is treating your board members as they want to be treated.

Diversity values different points of view. Diversity can be a real win-win situation, but you have to be prepared for the dynamics.

I recall one board where a liberal Democratic social worker often went head-to-head with a conservative Republican banker. The social worker thought the banker had no vision. The banker thought the social worker had no fiscal responsibility. But there was great trust and respect between them. Whenever an issue came up, they were the litmus test on whether or not it would float on both sides. Together, they had fiscal responsibility and vision. And it worked because they respected each other and the board respected them.

Diversity has enormous benefits.

- We can better understand our customers.

- We can compete for the best board members.

- It fosters innovation.

- We get a well-rounded perspective on decisions.

- We can better support the organization's goals and values.

- We can understand other organizations' cultures during collaborations and mergers.

- It reduces conflict between the board and employees.

- We can do the right thing, learn from others and have fun.

For diversity to work, we have to be willing to trust people who are different from us. One of the things we do with diversity is recruit people who move differently, who are a different color, who speak differently, or who have different perspectives – and we want them for all of those reasons. Then, we want them to act exactly like us when they get into the boardroom. That's not how it works, and it can all but kill any passion that board member has.

THE RECRUITING PROCESS:
The Passion Starts Here

So, how do we make sure all of our hard work thus far pays off in the recruiting process? Here's my suggestion on how to keep focused: Always remind yourself that you're running a business. It wouldn't be effective to hire a new employee without a well-planned and focused recruiting effort based on the mission of your organization.

Creating your dream team

If you could have anyone you wanted on your board, who would it be? Answer this question, and put it down in writing. I call this, "creating your dream team list." For example, I would want Paul Newman. He has his own foundation, works tirelessly in the community – and let's face it – the man is adorable.

Paul Newman aside, you should have your current board members submit their individual lists privately, and then distribute a master list to everyone, as an attachment to the meeting minutes.

Then, ask people to call you in private if they have any concerns about a potential candidate. You don't want to put people on the spot in an open forum if they have something critical to say about someone else. And sometimes, this information needs to be shared to avoid making a decision you might regret later.

Looking for passion in all the wrong places

Before I share ideas about where to find board members, let's talk about where not to find them.

First, stay away from relatives. (Some of you may already do that anyway…)

Let's go back to our AIDS organization example. Let's say you and I get our spouses on the board. Yours has a really big car to the deliver the meals, and mine makes a really great chocolate cake. But then, let's say you and I end up spending too much money (not that you and I would ever do that). Bottom line: they aren't the right people to evaluate whether or not we made the right decision.

You also don't want your competitors on your board. This is an easy trap to fall into. They have the same set of values, they understand your cause. They also may be going after the same funding. By all means, collaborate, form industry councils, have them serve on your advisory board, but remember, their group will always come first.

Finding the winners

Board banks. This is like a dating bureau for nonprofit boards. Some United Way offices have them. Sometimes it's the Junior League. And sometimes there are leadership programs with board banks, like Leadership Miami, Leadership New York or Leadership Philadelphia.

If you're not familiar with board banks, let me explain. Say you want to be on a board. You would go to the board bank and fill out a form, listing your skills and indicating the kind of groups with which you'd like to be involved. Then, a computer will match you with an organization that has corresponding needs. The great thing is, when you find someone through a board bank, you already know they have passion for your cause.

Community organizations. Check with groups like the Lions, Kiwanis or the Rotary. Tell them what you need and you'll find they're reliable in coming through for you.

Clergy. If you're interested in getting more Jewish board members, go to a local rabbi. If you're looking for African Americans, go to the minister of an African American congregation. The same goes for every religion and every type of board member. The clergy are marvelous in helping recruit.

Major donors. Keep an eye on who's giving and how much. Many of these people are delighted to give time and expertise along with their money.

Local companies. When you solicit funds from corporations, take the opportunity to solicit for board members as well. For instance, ask if there is someone in the marketing department who is interested in your mission, and who also might be interested in board service.

Real estate professionals. If you're looking for high profile board members, you want to connect with somebody who is selling expensive real estate to influential people. That way, you know who's coming to town, and you can get to them first.

Under your nose. I got a great board member one time from a United Way site visit. And then there are some who come through the committee structure, which is a great way to find out how dedicated people are to your cause and how well they follow through.

The bottom line: Don't discount any resources. I always like to say that the true test of someone's character is when you've carpooled with him or her for one year. That's really where you separate the good from the evil.

Keeping your eye on the fast track

Some of my colleagues call it stalking. I prefer to call it career tracking. Say, for example, you're following the activities of someone who heads a school board, the Convention and Visitors Bureau, or any large, visible group. When someone leaves a big commission like that, it sometimes leaves a big hole in their lives. That's the perfect time for you to swoop down and get that person.

You can also look for movers and shakers in the newspaper. Call them and ask if they'll have coffee with you. Find out when their term is up, and whether or not they're interested in your organization. If you can invite them to an event in your organization, do it. (Keep in mind, when you're courting high profile people, it's a good idea to bring them to special events that are associated with your group. It's never too early to start creating interest.)

Avoiding the pitfalls

Deal making. If you wake up one morning feeling like Monty Hall, go back to bed. The boardroom is no place to play "Let's Make a Deal."

So, what happens when you find this high profile person you really want, somebody like, well…Paul Newman. He says yes to your board, but then he says he can't come to any of your meetings. What do you do?

Here's the answer: there is a place for that person in your organization, and it's not at the board level. He can chair an endowment, be honored at your charity ball, or be on your advisory committee.

But if he can't come to the board meeting, he cannot be on your board. Trust me, if they say they can't show up, they won't. So it's not fair to the people you serve. And it's certainly not fair to a great guy like Paul Newman, who's going to get a bad rap even though he was straight with you in the first place

The other Paul Newman dilemma. Don't assume that having a well-known person on your board means you will have an active board member. These people are often willing to help, but they are often short on time. Again, there is a place for them, but it's not on the board.

Friendly competition. Once again, let's go back to our AIDS example. We may know of a great potential board member who's active in the AIDS community. Not only is she a dynamic person, but we can talk shorthand with her because she already understands what AIDS patients need. But here's the glitch: she could be up against us when it comes to funding. So, we may want to partner with her in some way, but we may not want her in our boardroom.

Misplaced experts. If you go after a board member with specific expertise, make sure he or she really belongs in the boardroom. This mistake often happens in medically-related groups. Folks who should be on an advisory committee are brought into a boardroom, where they decide on policy matters that really don't interest them.

Selective listening. Don't tune out your prospective board members the minute they say yes. You may miss out on important information that literally makes or breaks someone's success on your board.

I recall a conversation with a PR executive from a major metropolitan newspaper. She told me, "they do the same darn thing every time I'm on a board, they don't listen to me. I always tell them, if I'm on your board, do not expect me to do your PR, and I can't get you coverage in the paper. That's a conflict of interest."

But guess what? When she accepts board nominations, they ask her to do the PR. And it happens time after time after time. Now, she won't even join boards. It's a shame, because she has a lot to offer in other areas.

The big lie. All of us have our "big lies." For some of us, the big lie is that "you can wear that bridesmaid's dress again." But in the boardroom, it's this: "Serving on our board is not going to take much time." You and I both know that's not the case. So don't mislead your candidates to believe otherwise. You just set them up to fail.

Fear of rejection. Being afraid the word "no" can stop us from getting the board of our dreams. I've been turned down many times. But not once has anyone yelled at me and called me names for asking them to help. No one is ever insulted. After all, you're bestowing an opportunity and an honor, you're not imposing on them. It always needs to be perceived that way, and the perception starts with you.

The interview

Play matchmaker. In the interview situation, it's always a good idea to match your prospective board member with someone who shares a similar background and common interests. For example, if you want to bring a businessperson on the board, interview him or her along with several other business people who are already board members.

Ask the hard questions. The more we communicate upfront, the better. And that means asking candid questions to encourage honest answers.

The best recruiting interview I ever had was with a high profile gentleman who I had never met before. We went through, step-by-step, everything I could possibly want from him and why I wanted him. He eventually accepted our invitation, and he was great. He put me in contact with several high profile people, which is exactly what we needed.

The key is, he knew what was expected of him. And because of that, he became passionate for his role on our board, and he delivered beautifully.

Answer the hard question. Always be prepared and willing to answer this important question for your prospective board member: "What's in it for me?"

If, for example, you're working for the Juvenile Diabetes Foundation, and the potential board member has a sister with diabetes, this question probably won't come up. But if it's the child down the street, that's a different story. Then you have to show the candidate why the child with diabetes is more important to you than the child who's being abused. You have to be very clear on why it's important to join your board.

Bring a list of current board members. This action gives the candidate a chance to decline if there is someone on your board who presents an obvious conflict. Without the list, I once asked someone to join a board with his former spouse. Another time I got two people on the board who were suing each other. So much for our mission.

Let the candidate choose the time and place. I was so out of it one time I asked a commodity trader if he'd like to have lunch. Commodity traders don't eat lunch (I think they have I-Vs). The point is this: you may not understand the level of their professional and personal commitments, so always let your candidates decide.

Easy on the "stuff." Bring only brief, relevant information that will give the candidate a better understanding of your mission. In other words, no three-inch binders allowed!

Give thanks. Always send a timely thank-you note, along with other materials the candidate may have requested. In your note, be sure to outline why your group would be a good fit for your prospective board member.

The key in successful board recruiting is this: it's like any other courtship – to get to the next level, it has to be mutually attractive. And honesty is always the best policy.

The commitment

The time to learn what constitutes a "good job" is not when the board member is already sitting in the boardroom. That's why – once the board has voted in the new members, and they have verbally consented to board service – you should secure their commitment with a formal letter.

The board commitment letter helps you define the scope and expectations of board service before the candidate assumes the legal and moral responsibility of carrying out your mission. By minimizing surprises, you can prevent "the board dwindles." Plus, you can avoid the "moi" syndrome, which occurs when you ask your new board member to do something, and he or she looks at you in astonishment, and says, "Moi?"

At a minimum, your letter should include the following:

- Financial obligations – This is one of the most controversial aspects of board membership but, over time, I've learned that people are much more comfortable with guidelines. For example, you could mention a required $500 donation, or let the board member know that he or she will be responsible for securing at least two corporate donations.

- Meeting requirements – Be sure to mention the times, dates and places of upcoming meetings. Also mention the percentage of attendance expected, e.g. a board member in good standing must attend at least 60% of the meetings.

- Committee assignments – There are two kinds of board members: people who want to use the skills they use during the day, and those who want to do something completely different. You may assume an attorney wants to litigate on your behalf, when he or she really wants to organize special events.

- Committee expectations – Be clear as to what one can and can't do as part of a committee. For example, if you join the board of a small community ballet company, you're going to be asked to take tickets, sew costumes and paint scenery for the little ballerinas. But if you join the board of the New York City Ballet Company, not only are not you expected to, you're not allowed to sew costumes or paint scenery.

- Special event participation – This includes things like buying or selling a table for the dinner dance, bringing a foursome to the golf tournament, or any other required activity in which your board member must be involved.

- Board orientation and/or board retreat information – Include dates, suggested background reading, site visits, etc.

As a rule of thumb, send new board members two copies of the board commitment letter. Have them sign both copies and send one back to you. If the letter is slow in returning, call and make sure this is a good time and a good fit for the prospective member. If the person is having second thoughts, now is the time to know.

Here's another great thing about the commitment letter: It's an excellent opportunity for current board members to review their obligations and make sure they can keep their commitments during the upcoming term.

BOARD ORIENTATION:
Keep the Momentum Going

The board orientation is an extremely important part of the process. This is the point where new board members can really take pride in their involvement. They learn how to tell the story and, best of all, they create their own story and take ownership to your cause. That's what the orientation is really all about.

Board orientation can be done all at once, or on an individual basis. Orientation has different benefits in each case. Personally, I prefer the group approach. The advantage of bringing everyone on the board at the same time is that orientation takes place only once, meaning less staff and volunteer time.

On the other hand, you can individualize the process when you bring people on the board one-at-a-time. This way, the new accountant who joins receives more of a financial orientation, or the marketing manager focuses on the ways used to sell the agency to the public.

Board retreats

These are a great way to get people linked to your cause. For some groups, a board retreat will be an inexpensive, four-hour session in a church basement. Larger organizations with bigger missions may, by nature, require something more lavish. These groups may bring a facilitator to an out-of-town site, it may last for two or three days, and families may even be invited.

How you handle orientation is really up to your individual organization. But no matter what the format, the idea is to help people understand why they're in the room and what their board membership means to your organization.

Site visits

Say you're with an environmental group and you want to see the way an organic garden works. You could pile your board members in a van and talk about the bylaws on the way. Site visits are really easy with arts groups, too. On the other hand, with social service agencies, you have to be very careful. You're there to help, not exploit. Always remember that.

Board mentors

The board mentor is a personal resource and companion to the new board member during his or her early days on the board. The mentor explains why decisions are made, who the players are, and can even act as a host at the new member's first meeting.

When I joined Women's Self Help, my board mentor was fabulous. I felt so taken care of and so welcome into the organization. After the first meeting, she took me out for coffee and answered a lot of my questions. Then she wrote me a note and expressed her joy that I joined the board. I already believed in their cause. But after I spent time with my board mentor, they really had me.

Orientation rules to live by

Leave the notebooks at home. This is another part of the process where information overload becomes a temptation. Be selective. People need to know what they need to know, but they don't need to know 25 years of bylaws. For someone like me, here's what I want to know about the budget: Do I have one, and how much is left in it?

Have fun. I think board orientations have to be fun. When people are just sitting there and expected to listen and not experience, they won't learn as much, and enthusiasm can become defused in boredom.

* * * *

Every contact with a prospective board member has to be win-win from the very beginning. Anything we can do throughout the process to impress, inspire and enthuse our candidates improves our chance to have the board of our dreams.

And remember, while your new board member has a tremendous gift to give, he or she also has a lot to gain by serving in your organization. Not only do you offer recognition, status, contacts and power, you offer the priceless opportunity to support a cause you both value. And while we are running a business, it's the mission that really counts. That's where the passion lives.

Carol Weisman

Carol Weisman, president of Board Builders, is a speaker, author, trainer and consultant who specializes in volunteerism, fund raising and governance. Ms. Weisman has a Master's Degree is Social Work and a Masters Degree in Education from Washington University in St. Louis. She has served on 21 boards and has been president of 7.

Carol has worked as a medical social worker in pediatric oncology, hematology and neurology and neurosurgery at St. Louis Children's Hospital and Children's Hospital National Medical Center. She has published extensively on governance and volunteerism and is the author of "Build a Better Board in 30 Days: A Practical Guide for Busy Trustees" published by the F. E. Robbins and Sons Press. She is also featured in the PBS/Learning Institute Program on "Building a Board with a Passion for Mission."

In addition to traveling the world giving keynotes, training and doing board retreats, Carol is president of the Gateway chapter of the National Speaker's Association. She serves on the board of Women's Self Help, volunteers for the Learning Disabilities Association and is active in Toastmasters.

Carol lives with her sweet, long suffering husband of 22 years. Their oldest son is studying theater at New York University, the second son is an art student at Alfred University in New York State. The dog and cat are long gone, and Carol is thinking of letting the plants die.

Carol Weisman
Board Builders
48 Granada Way
St. Louis, MO 63124
phone: 888-500-1777 (toll free)
FAX: 314-991-3018
E-MAIL cewfer@aol.com

Does your board think
money grows on trees?

CHAPTER 2

Fund Raising for Newcomers to Nonprofit Boards

Charles D. Brown, Jr.

Newcomers to boards often regard development as an obsession with gathering money. Forget what you've been told and what you may have been led to believe. Fund raising is one of the most natural, enjoyable, satisfying, important activities you can undertake.

An old saying, oft repeated, is, "People give to people." It's a reflection of the fact that the best development efforts are relational, not transactional. What is important is giving people the affiliation they desire – in other words, treating people the way they want to be treated. If this is done, the dollars will take care of themselves. In fact, if this is done, you won't be able to stop the dollars coming in.

A common mistake is treating people the way WE want to be treated. It's not the same as treating them the way THEY want to be treated.

How do people want to be treated? The simplest way to find out is to ask them. But until you're able to do that, here's a guideline: People want to feel known, welcome, and important. And they also want to believe they are able to make a positive difference in support of activities that matter.

This chapter will explore some of the principles that contribute to fund raising success. Gaining a better understanding of these principles will make it possible for you to help create the environment and programs that will bring financial security to your organization.

What are these principles? Experience suggests you need to possess three things if you want to motivate people to give time and financial resources in support of not-for-profit activities. They are:

1. A worthy cause.

2. A personal commitment to the cause.

3. A philanthropic mind set.

A Worthy Cause

It is a revered custom in America to support the things that matter to us. We consider it a privilege to do so, and our government encourages philanthropic activity by granting tax exemption to organizations that serve the public good. Inviting others to join you in a meaningful activity is ennobling. In effect, you're saying, "This organization matters to me, and you matter to me, and I'd like you to be involved with me in the enterprise."

If you have agreed to give your time to an organization, you probably already believe it is a worthy cause. Reflect on why the organization was founded and, specifically, what difference it strives to make in the world. Is this something that is important to do? Will others find it a meaningful activity? If you can answer yes to these questions, you have a chance to persuade others they should invest in the organization's mission.

Drafting a "case statement" can help members of the board and other leaders organize their thoughts in formulating a compelling presentation. The case statement is a document that articulates the passion you and others feel for the organization, and it expresses the dream of a better future through the efforts of the organization. It also lays out the purposes for which funds are being sought. It is, in short, the world's window into the organization on whose board you serve.

Your Personal Commitment

What is the role of the board member when it comes to fund raising? You may very well become frightened by some well-meaning person citing the adage that a board member should "get, give, or get off," meaning that the job of a trustee is to raise money (get money for the organization, give money to the organization, or get off the board). It's not a view without some merit, but it seems to me it's looking through the wrong end of the telescope.

Most effective development operations are opportunity-driven, starting with where your organization is in terms of maturity (whether it's a start-up organization or is about to celebrate a major anniversary) and available resources (both in terms of personnel and financial support).

What is it about the organization's mission that interests you? Why have you agreed to be linked with the organization? Think about why you are involved and why the organization is important to you personally. You need to be able to feel passionately about it if you want others to support it. You will want to understand and be able to articulate the organization's needs. The personal investment you make in terms of understanding the organization will be important to prospective donors.

Additionally, your own financial commitment to the cause is critical. You need to be able to show that you have, relative to your means, made a gift as meaningful as the one you are asking others to make.

We express our values through the organizations with which we become involved and where we spend our time. But where we really come face to face with our values is in our checkbooks. Do you act on your beliefs and values by providing resources to advance them? Are you investing in the programs you say are important and which you want others to support? I've made a meaningful financial commitment to each organization for which I've sought support, including those that have employed me as a member of staff, and I've made a provision for those organizations in my will. I find it much easier to ask someone to elevate our cause among his list of philanthropies if I have done so myself.

A Philanthropic Mind Set

The third element essential to a successful fund raising program is the proper mind set. If the cause is important and if you yourself are committed to it both in terms of financial support and philosophy, you will be able to make a strong and persuasive case that others will respond to.

John D. Rockefeller Jr. probably received more appeals during his lifetime than any of us. Here's what he had to say about giving:

> *I have been brought up to believe, and the conviction only grows on me, that giving ought to be entered into in just the same careful way as investing, that giving is investing, and that it should be tested by the same intelligent standards.*

There is no reason to be shy about asking for support for your project or organization. As Rockefeller put it:

> *When a solicitor comes to you and lays on your heart the responsibility that rests so heavily on his; when his earnestness gives convincing evidence of how seriously interested he is; when he makes it clear that he knows you are no less anxious to do your duty in the matter than he is, that you are just as conscientious, that he feels all you need is to realize the importance of the enterprise and the urgency of the need in order to lead you to do your full share in meeting it; he has made you his friend and has brought you to think of giving as a privilege.*

I like to think that fund raising is the monument business. Nearly everyone has a basic desire to make a positive difference in the world and to leave some kind of mark to indicate his or her presence here. How do you want to be remembered? What kind of mark do you want to leave behind? You can make a positive difference through support for the organization you're involved with, and you're offering others an opportunity to make a positive difference through your organization, too.

It is often noted that John Harvard's body is buried in South Carolina, but his monument is in Cambridge, Massachusetts. Where will your monument be?

The Harvest Is Plentiful, but the Laborers Are Few

People involved with fund raising often want a cookbook solution to the problem. They are bored by the details; they just want the "recipe" so they can get to it. Regrettably, there's no sure-fire recipe for raising money successfully because every organization is different and the climates within which they operate are different. Fund raising isn't like baking a cake, where you add this to that and get a good result each time. It's more like painting. Or gardening. Gardening, now there's a useful metaphor.

The gardener's work, like that of the development officer, consists largely of planning, preparation, and cultivation. The time for harvesting the fruits of one's labor is relatively brief compared to the larger season, and although the harvest may be the raison d'être for the garden, the gardener nonetheless focuses primarily on cultivation, allowing the fruit to develop. That's because the role of the gardener is not to produce the fruit, but to create the conditions that will allow the fruit to mature. As one Eastern philosopher has put it, "The flower comes by itself." Given the right conditions, the flower will grow; and given the right conditions, people will want to give of time and resources to make a positive difference in the world. It isn't up to us to make it happen, but rather to create the conditions wherein it can happen.

Planning is the fundamental task for development, as well as for the gardener. Planning begins with an assessment of the needs of the community; only then can one determine the proper layout of the garden whose produce will meet the need. Planning doesn't end with making a plan, however. Each day's assessment of progress and needs of the garden suggests new measures or modifications to the existing plan.

There are many threats to a successful harvest, among them pests and pestilence and too little – or too much – of any essential ingredient. *But the greatest threat to yield is neglect.* We've all seen what happens when someone who is ignored by the institution for years is suddenly asked to make a gift bigger than he has ever contemplated. Nurturing is most effective when it begins early and continues without significant interruption.

One cultivates, and sows, and cultivates, and nurtures, and cultivates some more, bringing all one's skill and talent to the purpose at hand. And, believer or not, one prays. This is not a cheap play for insurance; it is an act beyond rationality, centered in the knowledge that our work binds us to something larger than ourselves and gives meaning to our lives. Having done all one can do, one feels compelled to reach out beyond human endeavor, to invoke the mysteries of creation and life.

No one knows better than the gardener (except maybe the development staff) that success is not guaranteed. After all one's efforts – and with luck – the harvest may vindicate the effort required to produce it. The time for harvest soon passes, however, and the yield is measured against expectation. If it is particularly bountiful, jubilation; if not, disappointment. In either case, the gardener's work begins anew, for one never finishes in the garden.

Getting Started

Let's examine some basic strategies for nurturing an individual from uninvolvement through support in fund raising initiatives; then you can begin to think more specifically about creating a program that will make sense for your organization.

Much has been written about the "solicitation cycle" or "cultivation cycle," and people who write about fund raising emphasize different components. I would suggest that the basic components are these: *identification, information, cultivation, involvement, solicitation, and stewardship.* Some development practitioners would expand the list and include things like the rating of a prospect's capacity to give, but I prefer to look at the relationship from the point of view of the prospective donor rather than that of the institution.

Identification

Like a good gardener, we'll start with recognizing the need to develop a plan – in this case, a fund raising plan. It's important, first, to be sure of one's target audience: Who can give to your organization? Who will?

Most support will come from individuals, foundations, corporations, and various government agencies. By far the most money given for philanthropic or charitable interests in America comes from individuals, and it makes sense to think individuals are likely to be your best supporters. You may discover in your research on individuals that an interested person is affiliated with a foundation or a corporate funding arm, and you can then pursue that connection.

As for individuals, whom do you know? Start with your friends – and friends of friends. Assume that people are already supporting worthwhile causes, and if you suggested they join you in supporting a cause that matters, you wouldn't be asking them to do anything they aren't already happily doing. Wouldn't they like to know about an organization in which you're so interested that you give time – that most precious asset – as well as money?

Take a look at lists of supporters of organizations with missions similar to yours, and develop a list of names for a direct mail effort. It may be that you have trustees or friends who have access to these individuals. You can get donor lists from annual reports of organizations, from playbills, and from fund raising auctions and galas for nearly any charity in your community merely by asking.

Organize a "Rolodex Meeting" for your board, where everyone brings his or her marketing list, holiday card list, or alumni list.

The individuals your organization serves (and their families and friends) are obvious possibilities as potential supporters. People who sell to your constituents should also be added to the list. This is particularly important for disease-related charities and hospitals.

Don't feel overwhelmed by the number of prospects out there. I thought of saying that everyone in America is a potential donor for you, it's just that some are more likely to support you than others. In fact, we live in a global economy, and we are a nation of immigrants. Your parent company in Bonn or your great uncle in Bombay may also be interested in your organization's mission.

Aim to make an incremental improvement in your list of possible supporters. See if you can add 100 names to your mailing list, to start. Or see if you can find a way to double your mailing list. At the same time you are expanding your list of prospects, you will be trying to improve the ratio of prospects who become donors; and once they become donors, you can focus on getting them to upgrade. If you aim for incremental improvement in each area of your fund raising effort, you can keep the tasks manageable and still make real improvement.

Most foundations give within a fairly narrowly described area, either geographically or programmatically. You may be able to locate a foundation that provides support to organizations in your state with missions like yours, and it would be worth checking this out. Foundations generally give start-up money for new organizations, programs, or initiatives, as opposed to general operating support. They are trying to maximize the impact of the funding they give; that is why they circumscribe support and why they are generally loath to give to operations. They want to prime the pump, as it were, but then they leave it to others to keep funds flowing. As you can imagine, funders receive requests for many more projects than they could possibly undertake, even if each one were deemed critical.

One of the best resources for getting information on grantmakers' interests and requirements for submitting requests is the *Foundation Directory*. It is available at many libraries and can be purchased directly from The Foundation Center, 79 Fifth Avenue, New York, NY 10003-3076 (see their Web site at www.fdncenter.org).

Before approaching any grantmakers, do your homework to ascertain their current interest and an appropriate level of support. Recognize that it may be easier to get a larger grant the second time around if you apply for a smaller amount and make something to show of their investment. Take note of the funder's interests, and try to find a way to match their interests with your programs.

For example, if a foundation is keen on public/private partnerships, explore whether there is a possibility to affiliate with a community organization or hospital or public school to provide a joint venture that would appeal to the funder.

Information

Having identified a target constituency, how do you approach them to begin the process of education and involvement? Religious institutions, retirement communities, service clubs and business clubs are possible places to start. Consider corporations, too: a fine-arts or performing arts organization might be able to do a presentation in the atrium of a corporate office building and thereby gain valuable exposure.

Most churches and synagogues have outreach programs, and it may be that they would be willing to sponsor support for your organization. Perhaps they could donate space, or perhaps they would allow you to make a presentation to their congregations for a special offering, or perhaps they would allow a member of the congregation (a person who is also involved with your organization) to talk about the work of the organization and ask those interested to become volunteers. You could also try to make friends with someone at a commercial real estate company and ask if they have a client who might like to donate space through the end of a troublesome lease.

Service Clubs like Kiwanis and Rotary (and business luncheon clubs) often have a speakers program, and their program chairmen are always looking for interesting presentations.

The point is to seek out opportunities to share your story and to invite people to become interested.

Three Steps to Gaining a Platform for Sharing Your Story

1. Call to see if the club or organization has a speakers program, and obtain the name of the program chairman.

2. Ask friends and trustees of your organization whether they know a member who could propose to the program chairman that your organization be invited to make a presentation. If it isn't possible to make a presentation, perhaps they would be willing to share your newsletter with their membership.

If you have no contacts within the club, don't hesitate to call directly. An introduction is useful, but not necessary.

3. Ask the club sponsor or program chairman to make a pitch for support – either to those present or to the club's board – as part of their outreach/ community service effort.

By sharing your mission with service-oriented individuals, you have a good chance to build a network of interested volunteers and donors.

Cultivation

Cultivation is the essence of building a personal relationship with an individual. As such, it is the most important part of the process of securing support for your organization. Kirk Unruh, director of donor relations at Princeton University, says, "Cultivation is not an event or even a series of unrelated events; cultivation is a process."

The process has to do with developing a special relationship. Major General Josiah Bunting III, superintendent of the Virginia Military Institute, puts it this way:

> *I mean "cultivation" that is not sporadic and haphazard, which is not fundamentally a matter of "having a drink" or "having dinner with" a donor, but which is a matter of becoming his friend, and exciting and sustaining his interest in some aspect of our work and needs here. It is a matter of earning trust, yes; but it is also a matter of regular, thoughtful communication about matters that have nothing ostensibly to do with "fund-raising;" it is a matter of discovering the donor's interest in certain things intellectual or musical or scientific or pedagogical or athletic, and basing at least part of a relationship on that interest.*

The importance of thoughtful communication is not unrelated to the importance of making people feel known, welcome, and important, which was cited at the beginning of this chapter.

One way to make someone feel known is to add a personal note to a letter or invitation that is being sent to her. Another way is to clip an article from a magazine or newspaper about a topic of interest to her and to send it to her with a note ("knowing of your interest in Spanish cuisine, I saved this restaurant review for you").

If the article bears on your organization, all the better; but it isn't necessary in order to make someone feel as though you took the trouble to think of what she would find interesting and then took the time to tell her.

When you encounter an individual at one of your events – whether it is a dinner or a sports outing or a reception – you can tell him how wonderful it is to see him, and make sure he is introduced to several other people so that he can carry on a conversation comfortably. We've all seen people at benefits for which they've paid a hefty admission fee, who don't seem to know anyone; no one seems to notice whether they stay or leave early. How much better it would be if you or another trustee were to stride up to the person and say, "John, I'm so glad you could join us this evening. I've been looking forward to having a chance to get to know you better, and I'd like to introduce you to some of our friends." That's how you can make someone feel welcome.

You make a person feel important simply by valuing her interest and showing her she matters to your organization. You look for opportunities to involve her with projects, and you seek her counsel as plans are being made for new activities. In short, you make her feel important by treating her the way she wants to be treated.

Soon after I returned to my alma mater as a staff member in the annual giving office, I attended a lecture on Shakespeare given by my favorite English professor. When I encountered my colleague Jerry Horton on the way back to the office, I was beaming. He asked what I was up to, and I told him I'd just been to a fabulous lecture given by a former professor. I said it made me feel like I was in college again, with a world of possibilities before me. The experience was tremendously inspiring. Jerry asked me if I'd told the professor or written him a note to let him know how much the lecture had meant to me. The thought hadn't occurred to me, and I said, "No. Should I?" Jerry responded, "Don't you think he'd like to know?"

It doesn't do any good to remember that you left the oven on when you headed out for vacation if you don't go back to turn it off. Likewise, there's little virtue that comes of thinking of someone if you don't let her know. You don't have to write a long letter of deathless prose or even trouble to make a phone call. A brief note will suffice to let the person know you're thinking of her and, in turn, to put yourself in her thoughts.

- "Jane, I was reading through my journal on vacation and came across your name, recalling our last visit, and I wanted to check in to see how you're getting along."

- "Ward, in conducting a reference check the other day, I spoke to a man named Flanders who used to work for your company. He remembered you and was hopeful you would remember him."

- "Frank – we've been thinking about how thoughtful you were to phone the other day to say hello . . . ."

One way to remind yourself to be in touch with someone is to ask yourself the question, "Don't you think she'd like to know?"

The art of cultivation is doing what comes to mind, *as if it mattered.*

Involvement

It's important to meet people where their interests lie. To do that, it's helpful, if you can, to get to know something about them. There are many resources in print available at your local library, including *Who's Who, Who Was Who, Who Knows Who, Dun and Bradstreet Reference Book, Standard and Poor's Directory, The Directory of Directors, Standard and Poor's $1Million Directory of Public and Private Companies,* and the *Social Register.* It may be that your prospect isn't listed in any of them, and that's no cause for worry – many of America's most generous donors aren't listed in any of them. At this stage, you're just trying to find out all you can about a person's activities, through which you can make inferences about his or her interests.

National news sources that may be useful for additional information include the *New York Times, Forbes, Fortune,* and *Town & Country.* Local sources include the local newspaper, business journals, and organization newsletters.

Among the best sources of information about an individual are the correspondence and personal interaction he has had with your organization. In the case of a new grassroots organization, there may be little in the way of correspondence. But this is something to pay attention to for the future. A "donor file" would help keep track of the relationship between the individual and your organization, so from now on, resolve that your organization will <u>keep everything</u> you send to or receive from any individual. And every time anyone from your organization has a conversation or a meeting with an individual, a brief report on the conversation should find its way into the prospect's file.

Some people may recoil at the notion of a file of information being kept on their dealings with an organization. But it isn't very different from your keeping track of the names of friends' children on your holiday list – you want to stay up-to-date in your relationship, but you can't remember everything about everyone, so you write it down. The organization has many more people to keep track of than you or I, and the organization represents all the relationships any of its trustees have with any of its supporters. To serve the interests of the individual prospect and to ensure that the relationship moves ahead in an area of interest to the prospect, it is important to keep track of information.

The best source of information about a person's interests is, of course, the individual himself. I've always been amazed at how much people will tell you. People generally like to talk about themselves, particularly to someone who is interested in what interests them.

Be sure to identify tasks volunteers could do when they express interest, and ask them:

Would you be willing to

- Help us find space for our organization?

- Do clerical work for our office?

- Work on the benefit committee?

- Serve as a trustee?

- Consider sponsoring a part of our program?

- Help identify people who would be interested in our mission?

- Host a reception where we could share our story with people who might become interested?

Solicitation

I don't like the term "solicitation" because it implies I'm trying to get someone to do something; I regard myself as a facilitator, helping an individual accomplish something he wants to do. Let us use the word as shorthand, but when we use it, let us think of holding a gift discussion with someone rather than asking for something.

People are rarely, if ever, prepared to give the amount they "could" give, even after years of cultivation. Asking is itself a form of cultivation, and it changes the nature of the relationship. Success from the fund raiser's point of view should be how much a donor gives compared to what he'd have given if he had not been asked. In reality, you can't possibly lose if you merely ask.

I've heard many development professionals – smart people, well-intentioned, earnest – say they aren't ready to solicit so-and-so because he hasn't had enough cultivation. As though cultivation were some amount of basting that has to occur before the old bird is tender enough to carve, and as though you only get one shot at it.

Remember the metaphor of the garden, and pay attention to what I call the parable of the peas. Peas need to be planted early, and conditions have to be ideal from planting to harvest to get the maximum yield. But sometimes the weather doesn't cooperate, and because the gardener is engaged with other things, he doesn't get the peas in the ground when he should. So the time for harvest comes, but the peas aren't mature. Now he has to choose: He can take what harvest he gets, or he can wait until next year and hope to catch it just right, banking on a more abundant crop. The amount of harvest he'll get from this year's crop of peas – whatever the yield – is greater than what he'll get if he doesn't pick the peas.

Every gardener knows that many plants are stimulated to produce more when their fruit is harvested. How does this relate to
development? Philanthropy is a learned behavior, and we need to
begin to develop it among those who can become leading donors in
the future, even though they may not be able to fill that role at
present. Experience demonstrates that solicitation and sight-raising
– asking for more than a person normally gives – have a cumulative
effect on people's attitudes and practices of giving.

When you seek support from an individual, you're saying, in
effect, "I want to have a new relationship with you." When I served
on the staff of The Lawrenceville School, I was having a gift discussion with a prospective donor, who asked me, "What I really want
to know is this: When I make a gift and we shake hands, is that
handshake going to be a "hello" or a "good-bye"? I used to urge my
colleagues to think of the opportunity any gift affords us for distin-
guishing ourselves and enabling an individual to achieve his or her
goals. I would say, "Let someone give $25,000 to us and $25,000 to
Harvard, and let us knock him over with the difference he feels he
has made to our organization."

As General Bunting has it, "Active and giving devotion is
kindled not by fund-raising activities but by long friendships built
on admiration and trust and the expectation that those things will
continue."

People new to fund raising often cite being told "no" as their
greatest fear of soliciting. None of us likes rejection, and it's easy to
fall prey to taking the outcome of a solicitation personally, especially if you're personally invested in the enterprise. Let's try to reframe
the solicitation in a way that takes the fear out of asking.

As John D. Rockefeller said, the duty of giving is your prospect's,
just as much as the duty of asking is yours. That's where you should
focus your interest and energy: the duty of asking. The outcome
isn't your responsibility; it is your prospect's. Remember that the
purpose of the gardener is not to make something happen but to
create the conditions where the harvest can happen.

It's useful to think of soliciting as the beginning of a discussion with an individual, rather than the end of anything. Experienced solicitors know that "no" doesn't always mean you won't be able to get a gift. No can mean many things, including:

- "No, that amount isn't right for me in my circumstances."
- "No, I'm not interested in that particular project."
- "No, the timing isn't right for a gift of that amount."
- "No, you're not the person I feel should be asking me."

If you think of solicitation as beginning a gift discussion, and if you are intent on trying to help the individual find a way to make an appropriate commitment to your organization, you can take time to explore how you might turn the "no" into a "maybe" or even a "yes." Sometimes an individual needs time to think over a commitment, just as she would an investment. Try to discover before you leave some possibility for coming back to the prospect with more information or another idea that will be a better fit.

Sometimes, of course, "no" does mean that the individual cannot see his way clear to making a commitment to your organization. You have no way of knowing the other demands on his resources, and so you shouldn't take a refusal personally. Remember that if you have asked, you have done your duty. You're in the business of developing a long-term relationship with the individual, and there will be other opportunities – if you are creative and attentive – to discuss support. Make sure your parting after a refusal is amicable, as your good relations with the individual are far more important than the result of any gift discussion.

Stewardship

The word "stewardship" is often used interchangeably with "cultivation" to describe those activities that move an individual along the continuum from identification to giving. For purposes of discussion here, let's assume that stewardship has to do with telling the donor the use you have made of his investment, both in terms of the way the funds have been allocated or dispersed and the specific achievements the benefaction has made possible.

Stewardship begins with acknowledgment: an official thank-you that states the amount of the gift, the date it was received, and the purpose for which it was intended. It is, in effect, acknowledgment of a contract that the funds given will be used for the purposes the donor intended.

Every gift is important, and every gift should be acknowledged in a timely way. The sooner the better, and the more personal the better, but there is no excuse for more than three business days to pass before a formal acknowledgment is made to a donor. It may be necessary to send a formal receipt to meet this deadline, after which one can send a personal letter. But in any case, it is important to let the donor know that the gift has arrived safely. This is especially true in the case of gifts of securities, when the donor may have given instructions to his broker to transfer shares and is eager to know whether the transaction has been properly completed.

Stewardship is, of course, a form of cultivation. It has been demonstrated many times that our best prospects are those who have given before, thus it behooves us to make donors feel known, welcome, and important.

What better way to make a donor feel important than to act as if his gift really matters?

Combining stewardship with cultivation offers many opportunities to enrich the relationship. Suppose I send you a pepper plant as a gift for your birthday. With a little imagination and minimal effort, you can turn that gift into a wonderful expression of a meaningful relationship. You could first write a note or phone (why not do both?) to say thank you. Later, you can write to say the plant continues to thrive (as if it mattered). Later on, you can write to tell me it has flowered and has set fruit. You can let me know the fruit has matured and you've consumed some, putting others by for later enjoyment. You can write to tell me how lovely the peppers are in a jar of vinegar; you can say what vein of memory was tapped when you tasted the vinegar on the season's first greens. And all this from a mere pepper plant. Think of how much more could be made of a book fund or a scholarship or a grant for a social need.

Each of the six elements of fund raising that I've mentioned (identification, information, cultivation, involvement, solicitation, and stewardship) could be a separate chapter unto itself. This brief overview will provide you with a context for learning more about fund raising. Experience is the best teacher, and as you proceed to seek support for your organization, you'll become better at it. You'll become more comfortable asking others to join you, and you may find – as so many others have – that you actually enjoy it.

* * * *

Some of my **favorite quotations** having to do with money and fund raising:

"People more often need to be reminded than informed."
Henry David Thoreau

"The flower comes by itself."
Osho, <u>The Empty Boat</u>

"A feast is made for laughter, and wine maketh merry, but money answereth all things."
Ecclesiastes 10:19

"Make no small plans; they have no magic to stir men's blood."
Daniel Burnham, architect of
the first World's Fair in Chicago, 1893

"People have made at least a start at understanding the meaning of life when they plant shade trees under which they know full well they will never sit."
David Elton Trueblood

"Development is the discovering of shared values; fund raising is giving people an opportunity to act on their values."
Kay Sprinkel Grace

"The harvest truly is great, but the laborers are few."
Luke 10:2

"All you can do is all you can do."
Dorothy Parker

Charles D. Brown Jr.

The magic of Charlie Brown is how he makes you feel about yourself. You feel like you are the most fascinating person he's ever met. He is an intense, active and excited listener.

This gift has made him one of the top development officers in the country. Charlie received his B.A. from Princeton University where he later returned to serve as Associate Director of Annual Giving. At Princeton, he worked with leaders of 25 classes whose combined constituencies number 25,000.

The Pennington School was the next to benefit from Charlie's expertise. At Pennington he managed the restructuring of the board of trustees, the adoption of a new campus master plan and the establishment of a program in capital support including planned giving.

In 1991, Charlie joined the Lawrenceville Leadership Campaign for the Lawrenceville School. As campaign Director, he raised $125 million, the largest in the history of American boarding schools.

After a stint at A. T. Kearney, Inc., where he provided executive search services to nonprofit organizations, Charlie joined the staff of the Solomon R. Guggenheim Museum as the Director of External Affairs.

Charlie plays the piano and the cello. He is a board member for Meadowmount School of Music in Westport, NY and the Meridian String Quartet in NY, NY. Charlie is married to Robin Mamlet, the dean of admissions at Swarthmore College in Swarthmore, PA.

Charles D. Brown Jr.
Director of External Affairs
Solomon R. Guggenheim Museum
1071 Fifth Avenue
New York, NY 10128
212-423-3779 • 212-423-3640 Fax
cbrown@Guggenheim.org

Board members let Steve know in the worst possible way that his performance is somewhat sub-par.

CHAPTER 3

The Job of the Trustee

Katherina M. Rosqueta

The Buck Stops Here

Think of the critical issues facing our communities – education, violence, healthcare, hunger, environmental protection, civil rights, housing. Nonprofit organizations address them. Nonprofits fight for cures, shelter the needy, prepare our workforce, advocate for the disenfranchised, and celebrate human expression through art and music. They represent a rich, diverse, and dynamic sector of our society.

We look to nonprofits to help build strong communities that sustain us all. We look to certain community members to govern these important institutions.

Nonprofit trustees are community members who make sure that nonprofits work to benefit the public good. To do this, trustees wear many hats. They are compliance officers, guardians, policymakers and managers. They are called upon to be ambassadors, fundraisers, in-house consultants, and volunteer staff. Above all, they are volunteer leaders, stewards of our community well-being.

For all of us who have agreed to serve as nonprofit trustees, one thing is certain: In terms of accountability for the work of the agency, the buck stops with us.

Governance and Support

Trustee responsibilities fall into two categories: governance and support.

Governance responsibilities are the formal, legal responsibilities of trustees. This is the "serious" work of the board. As governing trustees, we represent the public's interest, ensuring that our agency is following the rules and serving the public. In our governance function, we help set direction, allocate resources, and frame policies. We ask questions like "Have we paid our taxes?" "What do we do in the face of welfare reform?" "Should we close our doors?" "Are we doing a good job?" "Does this program serve our mission?"

However, many of us join boards not because we want to ask the tough questions but because we like a particular agency's work and want to make a difference. We want to help an organization succeed and hopefully, along the way, meet new people and develop new skills. What's more, many of us are asked to join boards because an agency wants our help in very concrete ways.

Support responsibilities are the volunteer responsibilities we assume to help the organization get its work done. Rather than simply remain a judicious but detached governor, we act as the agency's most stalwart helper and loudest cheerleader.

As supporters, we raise money, deliver speeches, and tap connections on behalf of our agency. We lend our financial expertise to set up an accounting system. We lend our marketing expertise to produce a brochure or our human resources expertise to craft a personnel review system. When there are few or no paid staff, we translate for clients, manage volunteers, or stuff envelopes for a mailing. These functions are not, strictly speaking, the job of the nonprofit trustee, but they are in the spirit of the trustee's support responsibilities: Help when you can, however you can.

Governance Jobs

Governance jobs are those trustee jobs in which we ask the hard questions and then make sure there are good answers. There are four different types of jobs that we assume while wearing our governance hat: compliance officer, guardian of the mission, manager of the executive director, and policy-maker.

Trustee as Compliance Officer:
"Are We Following the Rules?"

SAN FRANCISCO–Thousands of dollars donated to the Well-Intentioned Agency (WIA) will never reach the homeless children donors thought they were supporting. A surprise audit uncovered mounting back taxes and a gross misuse of agency funds. Ignoring their own fiscal policies, members of WIA's board of directors steered agency contracts to their own companies and gambled thousands in aggressive investment schemes. — Community Newspaper

Funders, the media, the Internal Revenue Service and others serve as watchdogs for the nonprofit sector. But they generally don't step in until after a rule has been broken, a regulation disregarded, and common sense forsaken. When negligence, wrongdoing, and stupidity are discovered, the chorus is always the same: "Where was the board?"

Our job as trustees is to ensure that our agency is operating in compliance with all the rules and regulations that govern it. We are the internal compliance officers who monitor the agency (and ourselves!) on an ongoing basis.

Some of the questions we should ask as we monitor the *organization* are:

- Are we filing the required annual tax returns and payroll reports? (And is the information we're providing accurate?)

- Are we paying the required taxes on time?

- Are we observing the legal limits on lobbying activities and political electioneering?

- Do we have adequate liability insurance?

- Are we maintaining and observing written personnel policies, accounting procedures, and internal controls?

- Are we meeting the terms of our contracts and funder grant agreements?

Some of the questions we should ask as we monitor *ourselves* are:

- Are we scrupulously avoiding conflicts of interest? (Once we join a board, our primary loyalty is to the institution we serve and the public it serves. We hold community assets in trust and must act to benefit others, not ourselves.)

- Are we in compliance with our own organization's bylaws? (By-laws are the operating rules and procedures for a corporation. By-laws stipulate such items as minimum number of board members, selection procedure for board officers, frequency of meetings, and process for passing resolutions.)

- Does our composition reflect the diversity of perspectives, skills, expertise, and connections that will enable us to govern effectively?

This last question is critical in helping us carry out another governance job.

Trustee as Guardian of the Mission: "Are We Doing What's Right?"

"Two years ago, we began a huge capital campaign to open a hospice center for people dying of AIDS. Now, with new treatments and changes in the epidemic, funders and community activists are saying, 'We don't need hospice care; we need outreach to women and communities of color.' Do we continue building for a hospice facility?"
— *AIDS Agency Board Member*

"On the one hand, we know that the Internet has the capacity to reach more people than we could ever meet in person. On the other hand, we know people are more likely to volunteer when they feel connected to the person or agency asking. We have limited funds. Is our mission to involve more residents in community service better served by developing a comprehensive Web site or securing satellite office space at the public library?" — *Volunteer Center Board Member*

Just as the buck stops with us in terms of compliance, it also stops with us in terms of the mission. Whether an agency's mission is to end domestic violence, maintain safe drinking water, showcase modern dance, or educate a technology-savvy work force, our job as trustees is to make sure that the agency we govern is serving the public good with the resources it has.

The public has a right to expect us to act in its interest. Tax benefits to nonprofit corporations represent $30 billion each year . The sector as a whole represents more than $500 billion worth of revenue. In addition to tax benefits and income, nonprofits also receive contributions from the public in the form of in-kind donations and millions of hours of volunteer time.

The fundamental question for any trustee should therefore be: "Are we serving the public good with the assets it has given us?"

To answer this big question effectively, we must break it down into smaller questions:

- What is the agency's mission? Why is it important?

- What external factors affect our ability to fulfill our mission? (For example, are there funding trends, legislation, or scientific or technological developments that challenge us to change the way we think about our mission?)

- What internal factors affect our ability to fulfill our mission? (For example, do our program offerings and budget reflect the best allocation of resources to fulfill our mission?)

- Are there opportunities for collaborations that will better leverage our assets?

- What do we do well? What could we do better?

- Have we fulfilled our mission? Should we close? Should we merge?

Trustees seek answers to these and other questions during the process of developing a strategic plan. Once a strategic plan is in place, our job is to ensure that the strategic plan is implemented and modified as needed to best fulfill the agency's mission.

Trustee as Manager: Do We Have the Right Executive Director to Lead the Agency?

"I've served on three boards already. One thing I've learned: Before I join a board, I need to understand and feel comfortable with the relationship between the board and the executive director. Otherwise, it can turn into a real mess!"
— *Veteran Nonprofit Board Member*

Many nonprofit organizations (for example, Rotary Clubs, PTAs, alumni groups, soccer leagues, and sororities) do not have a paid executive to manage the agency. But for those agencies that do employ a paid executive, the relationship between the board and this chief staff person – often referred to as the executive director (ED), chief executive officer (CEO), or president – is critical.

Let's start with what the executive director is not. The executive director is not the employee of any one trustee. The executive director is not an assistant to the board.

The executive director is the person who hires and manages the agency's staff, pays the bills, and directs the programs. This person implements policies approved by the board and has management responsibility for all financial, administrative, and personnel matters related to the organization's business. As trustees, we hope to bring that magical combination of "work, wealth, wit, and wisdom" to an agency's work. However, it is the executive director who ultimately directs the operations of the organization.

The executive director is also the only staff person with whom we, as trustees, have any supervisory or managerial relationship.

In delegating the management of agency operations to the executive director, we are responsible for:

- Selecting the chief executive.

- Determining appropriate compensation and performance goals.

- Supporting the executive's work in attaining those goals.

- Reviewing the executive's performance.

- Coaching, encouraging, rewarding, disciplining, or firing the executive as needed.

To carry out this governance job, a board generally chooses a subcommittee of trustees to carry out the various functions associated with overseeing the chief executive. An executive committee is often responsible for ongoing support and review of the executive director's work. A personnel committee may outline a process for annual performance review and formal feedback, as well as make recommendations for compensation and merit pay increases that are in line with board-approved personnel policies. A search committee would oversee the recruitment and selection of a new executive director and make recommendations to the full board for a vote. Major decisions regarding the executive director's status – such as hiring or firing an executive director – would be determined by the full board with recommendations from relevant committees.

Many executive directors are professionals with as much managerial experience as their board members and usually, with more expertise in the organization's field than their board members. Some sit on the board alongside the volunteer trustees. The adage, "The board sets policy and the staff implements it," must be qualified to include the fact that in many organizations the executive director is best positioned to recommend policies to the board, who ultimately must approve them.

Trustee as Policymaker: What Should Guide Our Work?

"Employee salaries will be reviewed annually and adjustments made subject to the availability of funds and the performance of the employee."

  — *Personnel policy approved by the board*

"Employees who work our information booth at this year's Women's Conference will be reimbursed for expenses related to the conference."

  — *Staff policy outlined by the executive director*

To ensure that our agency is doing what is right, fair, legal, and effective, we approve written policies that help guide us and the executive director in making decisions and carrying out our respective duties.

Policies are developed at different levels. The executive director may recommend policies for board adoption. The executive director may work with a committee of trustees to research and draft policies. Trustees may research, develop, and ask for a board vote for adoption of policies. While the board ultimately approves the policy, it is important for trustees to consult with the executive director to make sure that policies can be implemented.

There are big policies and small policies. A policy regarding when employees take lunch is a small policy. A policy that there be 24-hour staffing of an emergency hotline is a big policy. The board is concerned with the big policies, those guidelines and systems that affect the entire organization and have the greatest direct impact on the fulfillment of the organization's mission.

The following are the types of policies trustees should make sure are in place, followed, annually reviewed for appropriateness, and modified when needed to adapt to changes brought on by an agency's growth and evolution:

- Organizationwide personnel policies.

- Investment policies.

- Financial oversight and internal control policies.

The board may also wish to adopt policies in response to certain important external factors. For example, when Proposition 187 was passed in California, some boards who serve primarily immigrant families passed a policy not to require proof of legal residency for emergency shelter or inoculations. The boards felt that their agencies needed such a policy to serve their clients. When caller ID technology was launched, some boards of organizations requiring client confidentiality, such as rape-crisis hotlines, made a point of approving a policy to block caller ID on their phonelines.

Boards may also need to adopt policies to guide themselves. For example, adoption of a conflict-of-interest policy helps make clear to all trustees what they must avoid once they agree to serve on the board.

Support Jobs

Support jobs are those trustee jobs in which we work to make sure our organization is successful. In supporting our organization's work, we have four primary jobs: ambassadors, fundraisers, in-house consultants, volunteers.

Trustee as Ambassador:
Building Positive Community Relations

"What do I want? I want board members who carry our brochures in their briefcases, who tell everyone – their friends, family, the guy they're waiting in line with, the editor of the newspaper – about this great organization they volunteer for!"
— *Board Chair, Community Foundation*

By serving on a board, we send a powerful message to the rest of the community: "This organization is so important that I am willing to take responsibility for it in addition to my family, my career, and my other commitments."

As trustees, we are in a unique position to serve as ambassadors. Unlike staff (who are paid by the organization) and clients (who receive services from the organization), we receive no explicit compensation or benefit from our agency's work. When we serve as spokespeople for the organization, we speak not out of self-interest but out of belief in the value of our agency.

Trustees are community members who come to the boardroom with affiliations to other organizations and groups. We are connected to families, businesses, neighborhood associations, alumni societies, churches, and more. It has been said that one way to measure the value of a board is by looking at the "sum of its connections." These connections not only inform our perspectives but also represent an important network of potential community support for our agency.

When we wear our governance hat, we affirm the value of our agency's mission and oversee allocation of resources accordingly. When we wear our support hat, we make sure the rest of the world understands the value of our agency's mission.

There are many ways to serve as an ambassador for an agency: from speaking before large assemblies to discussing the agency's work over coffee with the local minister, from designing a year-long public relations campaign to passing out brochures at a conference table, from walking at a march against AIDS to fielding questions from the press. In all cases, our job is to build positive relations between the nonprofit organization and the larger community.

One of the payoffs of good community relations is that if others feel good about our organization's work, they are more likely to contribute in-kind donations, volunteer time, and, most importantly, money.

This takes us to another support job of the trustee: Fundraising.

Trustee as Fundraiser:
Helping Ensure Adequate Resources

"I'd rather stick a needle in my eye than ask for money."
— *Trustee No. 1*

"If you're not willing to help fundraise, then why are you on the board?"
— *Trustee No. 2*

The vast majority of nonprofit boards expect that individual board members will be involved in fundraising for the organization. As one corporate employee aptly put it, "The difference between serving on a for-profit board versus a nonprofit board is that when you serve for a for-profit, they pay you. When you serve on a nonprofit, you pay them!"

Since we, as trustees, provide direction in policies and programming and often approve the budget, we are responsible for ensuring that there are adequate resources to carry out the organization's work. One way we can do this is by fundraising.

Effective fundraisers know that you can't ask anyone to give – whether the potential donor is a foundation, a corporation, a government office, or an individual – unless you, yourself, have given. Indeed, there are few statements more compelling to potential donors then the statement that there is 100% giving on your board.

By making a personal financial contribution, we send a clear message, "This organization is worth donating to."

There are almost as many ways to view trustee roles in fundraising as there are nonprofit boards. While some organizations do not expect their members to be involved in fundraising at all, most expect that trustees will be involved in one of the following ways:

- Personally significant contribution (sliding scale): Trustees are expected to make financial donations that are "personally significant" to them. Consider your own personal financial resources and ask yourself what amount would be the largest charitable contribution you would be willing to make this year. Remember that this is not just another contribution. As a trustee for your organization, you have assumed a special leadership position that you have not assumed for other worthy causes.

  One way to think about your personal gift is to consider what a peer would consider generous. In other words, if a peer – a friend, colleague, business associate, or family member – found out what you donated, they would be likely to tell you "That is a generous gift you gave that organization."

- "Give or get": Each board member is expected to give (of his or her own personal resources) or get (by selling tables for an event, organizing a fundraiser, or writing a solicitation letter to potential donors, for example) a certain amount each year.

- Minimum contribution: Each board member is expected to give a minimum contribution, which can be as small as a $25 membership fee or as large as tens of thousands of dollars.

- Participation in fundraising activities: Each board member is expected to participate in some aspect of fund development. This may include identifying potential donors, writing or editing a grant proposal, coordinating a fundraising luncheon, accompanying staff on donor calls, introducing the executive director to potential contributors, or soliciting in-kind donations.

Trustee as In-House Consultant: Giving It for Free

"I know we need to fundraise. I'll sell the tickets and make the donation to meet our goals. But, frankly, my biggest satisfaction comes from lending my skills. I'm trained as a CPA. I know some people would say, 'Why would you want to spend more time being an accountant.' But it's when I'm using my accounting and finance skills that I feel most like I'm making a difference. That's when I'm really giving of myself." — *Board Treasurer, Theatre Company*

While the need to raise enough money to meet the budget is an urgent one for many nonprofits, we can and should be seen as more than potential bankrollers of the organization's activities.

Another way to think of a nonprofit board is as a potential "brain trust" for the organization. Trustees often bring training, skills, expertise, and experience that a nonprofit could not afford to bring onto its paid staff. The agency that cannot afford a finance department can look to the CPA on the board. The agency without a personnel department can seek help from trustees who are human resources professionals. The nonprofit that does not retain counsel on staff can look to lawyers on the board to identify legal implications of their work.

The role of in-house consultant can be extremely rewarding. Many of us join our boards because we feel we have specific skills or experience to lend. Many trustees feel their biggest personal impact when they are volunteering something they feel uniquely qualified to give.

Especially in newer, smaller organizations, trustees lend programmatic expertise, as well as management expertise. A new counseling program seeks advice from trustees who are psychologists and social workers to develop age-appropriate programs for abused children. A meal-delivery program seeks advice from nutritionists, restaurateurs, and management consultants to determine the most efficient way to prepare and deliver nutritious meals to the city's homebound. Many organizations would simply not be able to do their work effectively without trustee consultants.

Trustee as Volunteer Staff: "How Can I Help?"

"With only two full-time staff and a budget of $250,000, they need help. I've got time, energy, and I respect what they do. If it will help to have me set up tables, edit a grant proposal, or spend a half an hour licking stamps, you bet I'll do it. I'm not one of those stuffy, board-member types."
— *Board Member, Childcare Agency*

Large numbers of nonprofits have no full-time paid staff. (In California the figure is estimated to be 75%.) The organization is the board, and we, as trustees, are responsible for implementing the activities of the agency.

This is especially true for new grassroots organizations in which we not only hold the fiduciary responsibility for the organization, but are also the agents for delivering services and managing the day-to-day administrative tasks. This can be an exciting time to be a trustee: you are working to build a new organization and realize a new vision. It can also be an exhausting time. The work needed to launch a new organization can be overwhelming, and switching from our "governance" hat to our "support" hat can be time-consuming and very confusing.

Generally, the more established an organization is, the more paid staff resources are at its disposal, and the more likely we, as trustees, will focus primarily on governance duties, public relations, and fundraising and less on volunteer support.

* * * *

Few activities can be more challenging, frustrating, and rewarding than serving on a nonprofit board. The benefits for those of us who serve are many: an opportunity to develop skills (and learn new ones), to enhance our leadership capacity, to expand our networks, to deepen our understanding of our community, and to work alongside people we would otherwise never meet to fulfill a mission we believe in.

Serving as a trustee is also a chance to leverage our volunteer involvement. One woman who served as both a tutor and a trustee of a local educational agency describes it this way: "When I volunteer as a tutor, I get satisfaction from seeing the progress in the young girl I work with. When I volunteer as a trustee, I know that the time I spend in strategic planning and fundraising is going to help the five hundred girls our agency tutors each year."

For those of you who are reading this chapter because you've already been elected to a board, congratulations and thank you for assuming such an important role in our communities. And for those of you are contemplating joining a board, thank you for your interest in making a difference. The nonprofits who seek your leadership are a vital part of our community and could not do their work without your help.

Katherina M. Rosqueta

What's most striking about Kat is the intelligence and thoughtfulness with which she approaches every subject, whether it's nonprofit governance, ethnic diversity or the challenges of interfaith marriage.

Katherina M. Rosqueta was the founding director of Board Match Plus, a collaborative venture between the Support Center for Nonprofit Management and the Volunteer Center of San Francisco. Board Match Plus recruits and prepares new candidates to serve on boards and provides educational, training, and consulting services to support those already serving as trustees. In particular, the program has focused on the effective recruitment and support of trustees from communities of color.

A graduate of Yale University, Kat's background includes her community affairs and volunteer management experience with Wells Fargo Bank's Corporate Community Development Group; research for Co-op America's *A Socially Responsible Financial Planning Guide*, development of a corporate mentoring model for diversity for Wells Fargo Bank and Hewlett Packard; and training in employee involvement programs, fairlending compliance, and nonprofit board development.

Kat's extensive community service experience includes chairing the Bay Area Week of Caring and serving as president of the board of La Casa de las Madres, San Francisco's oldest and largest shelter for battered women and their children.

Katherina M. Rosqueta, Director
Board Match Plus
1160 Battery Street, Suite 70
San Francisco, CA 94111
ph. 415.982.8999 • fax. 415.399.9214
E-mail. kat@boardmatchplus.org
www. boardmatchplus,org

CHAPTER 4

Making Nonprofit Board Meetings Work – or Averting Nonprofit Board Meeting Meltdown!

David M. LaGreca

Midway through the meeting – which looked like it would last at least two and a half hours – I realized that I was planning my schedule for the next week, writing mental notes to confirm plane reservations and wondering why I ever got involved with this group. Final note to myself – plan an out of town trip next month on the day of the meeting! — Sue

Boy did we get things done tonight! A decision about the direction of our fund raising efforts for the next three years, a presentation on an education conference co-sponsored with a local hospital and the first of two discussions on our advocacy policy – all in 90 minutes. We even spent the first 20 minutes sharing our personal reasons for being on this board with two newly elected members! — Jack

We've all attended board meetings and walked away feeling that we had wasted precious time. But just what is it that makes Sue's experience so radically different from Jack's? **Board meetings – defined as volunteer board members spending time together making governance decisions for the future of the organization** – can have a major impact on the success of the board. It is up to those who plan, lead, and participate in nonprofit board meetings to ensure that the impact is a positive one.

Why meet?

The very question sounds odd, but why should nonprofit boards meet? The answer sounds equally odd – **to focus on making critical decisions**. This guideline should be applied at every step of the board's life – from scheduling meetings to strategic planning. How does this board activity further the organization's mission? It's a simple reality check that can keep a board on the right track.

Meetings are hard work – and ensuring their productivity is the hardest work of all. The following advice is based on more than 15 years of personal nonprofit board service – and years of experience working as a consultant to nonprofit boards of directors.

Board Leadership: The Chair

The chair (some nonprofit boards call the leadership position "President") is critical in achieving effective board meetings. The chair's role is to lead, orchestrate, move, cajole, and push nonprofit boards and board committees into acting in the best interests of the nonprofit. This leadership role has been described in various ways:

- *Orchestra conductor* – so that the brass section does not drown out the reeds.
- *Lion tamer* – ensuring that the end product is worthwhile and safe!
- *Nurturer* – making sure that each volunteer on the board receives what she or he needs to continue to be of value to the organization!

Sounds like tough love, huh?

I view my role as chair as balancing control and chaos – my preference is to begin a meeting with all my ducks in a row – but always prepared for someone or something to get out of line!
                                                                    — Susan[1]

---

[1] All quotes are from board members.

While the chair has an important role in the success of non-profit board meetings, all board members are responsible for what happens at meetings. The unique peer group called a nonprofit board can succeed only if all members have the interests of the nonprofit foremost in their minds.

The following activities – based on the accumulated wisdom of many individual chairs and board members – are necessary for effective governance:

- Planning
- Working
- Learning
- Deciding
- Connecting
- Speaking
- Acting
- Enjoying

I. PLANNING

Axiom 1
Have a plan – no plan, no meeting!

Beginning with the first glimmer of a thought to call a board meeting, planning is the most crucial element. Try stating the goal of the meeting in one sentence (if you can't, question your rationale). For example, our board/committee is meeting to:

- Review and accept next year's budget.
- Conduct the annual performance review of the executive director.
- Map out next year's calendar of special fundraising events.

Each meeting – committee or full board – should have an agenda. Good agendas label things – and give board members information about the relative value of each item. Some things can be labeled *for discussion*, still others can be labeled *for decision* or *update*. Planning for a successful meeting often requires a meeting of some combination of the board chair, the executive director and the executive committee.

Try this!

Get your board meetings on board members' "calendars" first, by establishing meeting dates at the beginning of the year. Periodically reconsider the time and place of the meeting – for example, perhaps the current board members would find an early morning meeting more convenient than the luncheon session that former board members preferred.

Why read this stuff? ....We receive a meeting agenda the day before each board meeting. It always has the same five points – with no indication of what the "real" agenda might be. Last month, I arrived at a meeting to discover that the real issue was hidden under the label "New Business" – the chair wanted immediate approval of a 10 percent raise for the executive director. We were supposed to discuss this and make a commitment that night. Luckily, we stopped that...
— Sally

DANGER: Board Packets

In interviewing hundreds of board members over the past seven years, it is clear that a common complaint focuses on the dreaded *Board Packet!* Often arriving too late, the packet is variously described as *unreadable* (material sent without explanation of how it fits into the agenda), the *wrong stuff* (one organization sends a copy of its general ledger for the month to each board member – which even members of the finance committee find confusing), *without board issue content* (a glowing "everything is fine" report). An easy guideline to follow: every sheet of paper in the board packet should be self-explanatory. A good board packet contains background information — not reports to be read at a meeting. Aim for one sheet of paper per committee report!

II. WORKING

Axiom 2
Sitting on a board means work – by board members and not just the staff.

Meetings are work – pure and simple. Nonprofit board meetings entail work on the part of board members. Non-working/non-participating board members are oxymorons!

Effective meetings require work before – and focused attention during – the meeting, as well as follow-up. Prior to meetings, the chair and the executive director do the major work (materials need to be collected from various members – sometimes requiring what one board chair calls "hectoring" board members – and then reviewed). During the meeting every board member needs to help keep the work of the board moving forward. After the meeting, each member must work to achieve agreed upon commitments.

Try this

One organization spends 30 minutes at its first fall meeting divided into committee groupings. Each committee gathers the work materials, such as minutes and reports, shared with other board members during the previous year. At the end of the 30 minutes, the committee must decide to affirm, replace or alter its materials for the coming year. In a brief feedback session with the full board, the committee also presents a qualitative assessment of its work during the last year, complete with such comments as "unrealistic expectations," "did nothing," "provided good input for the organization." Some board members report that this is actually fun!

DANGER: Doing Your Own Stuff!

In many instances – board meetings generate work for the staff of the nonprofit. However, the board must ensure that it does its own work! Boards should:

- Schedule their meetings.

- Take their minutes.

- Make their reports at board meetings.

- Follow through on their commitments between meetings.

- Evaluate their performance.

...some of my fellow board members act as though the staff exists to implement their wisdom! They dream up stuff at meetings and don't think about it until the next meeting when they expect an update. It's embarrassing at times. I thought I was on this board to contribute my time and energy...

— Malcolm

III. LEARNING

Axiom 3
Give board members a chance to learn
something at each meeting.

Board members are volunteers and on-the job training is a hallmark of successful organizations. Try highlighting an aspect of your program at each board meeting. One organization includes a regular agenda item called FYI. Each month, the board receives a briefing on a different aspect of the organization's programming. Another organization asks board members to visit at least two program sites each year – and schedules board meetings at these sites with tours of the facility before the board meeting. Yet another organization sends an article on the board's role (in fundraising or fiscal accountability, for example) in each board packet and includes a short discussion of the article on the agenda. Knowledgeable board members are happy ones – and more apt to find new ways to assist the organization.

Try this

At the beginning of each fiscal year, have the board decide what program activities it would like to know more about over the coming year. With some experience, the board can even decide how it would like to be briefed. For example, one board decided that it wanted to know about the program staff as well as the programs and asked the Executive Director to have a different staff member attend each full board meeting and do a fifteen minute presentation.

...we recently invited a member of our cultural advisory board to update us on the current state of public funding for the arts. Our board is constantly focused on our own finances – and hearing an overview of what the entire cultural community is facing helped us feel better about our own accomplishments – as well as renew our commitment to the task at hand...   — Lola

---

IV. DECIDING

Axiom 4
Make sure that a decision about something is made at each meeting.

Each meeting – committee or full board – should include at least one decision. This sounds easier than it is. Often board meetings become a time for reports to be read at people. Remember, getting board members to come to meetings depends on each member's answer to a basic question: "Will we decide something at this meeting that requires my input, and will my attendance make a difference?"

For complex matters, a well thought out decision-making process can be critical to the decision's outcome. A large children's social service agency was faced with renovating a 40-bed psychiatric inpatient center. The treasurer set out a six-month decision process that ended with the board's deciding to seek long-term bond financing. The process allowed the board to educate itself concerning this complex financing arrangement, confer with a broad range of experts, review its options and ultimately make a sound decision for the organization's future.

Try this

Establish the habit of including the same item on the agenda for two consecutive meetings. For the first meeting, the topic can be labeled *for discussion*. At the end of the discussion, the chair can ask the appropriate committee to re-present the topic *for decision* at the second meeting. This curtails discussions that go on for months while ensuring that the board has the information it needs to make a good decision.

...the board I sit on approaches decision-making from two extremes – either all the decisions are made before we arrive at the meeting (by the Executive Director, the Chair or who knows!) or we spend two hours deciding on the color of the tablecloths at the annual dinner. Either way – I begin to wonder why I rushed to leave the office early to get here.

— Donna

DANGER: Bad Decisions Poorly Made

The board of one elderly services organization decided at its quarterly meeting to expand its program by applying for a state grant to do job training for teenagers. The idea was presented, discussed and decided on in 30 minutes. A year later, the organization was still trying to get past this ill-advised decision.

V. CONNECTING

Axiom 5
Allow board members time to get to know one another at each meeting.

Part of the fun of nonprofit board service – and a major factor in retaining good board members – is the opportunity to meet people committed to the things that are important to us. Meetings should ensure that board members have time to talk with – and get to know – each other. Some boards do this by serving something to eat before or after each meeting, allowing people to spend some time together.

Another board expects each board member to attend the organization's twice-a-year fundraising events – not to guarantee ticket sales – but to ensure that board members socialize with one another and work as a team in a non-meeting setting.

Successful boards understand that time spent helping the board members know one another will pay off fourfold!

Try this

Once a year, one board spends time at its orientation meeting (which all members are expected to attend) asking individual board members to share with the group why they wanted to serve on this board – or why they continue to serve. This board invites the entire staff to participate in the session. It's a simple exercise that goes a long way toward helping each person understand everyone's commitment and dedication.

...I was beginning to question my value as a member of my board, when the chair asked each of us at the last meeting to share our original reasons for joining the board. Listening to my fellow board members, I realized how committed they were and why I still wanted to contribute to the board's work...

— Thomas

VI. SPEAKING

Axiom 6
A happy board is one where each board member speaks at each meeting – but not too little or too much!

Each board member should be encouraged to contribute at each meeting, but some board members may need help to interact. Remember, each board member comes with her/his previous experience with working as a team and group decision making. For example, the board member invited on the board for his knowledge of the local community and its political and social networks may be cowed into silence by the presence of several business executives. Conversely, the business executive – working in a hierarchical company, where giving and taking orders are commonplace, may not be accustomed to being openly challenged by her peers and may react with silence.

The peer structure of a nonprofit board requires all board members to participate if the organization is to benefit from their collective experience and wisdom. The role of the board chair is crucial in achieving this goal. For example, the chair can invite silent board members to talk by directing questions to them or soliciting their input on topics where their particular input can be valuable. The chair can also keep track of those who are not participating and encourage them privately.

Try this

The chair or executive director can keep a "chirp list." To ensure that each board member contributes to moving the discussion forward, a simple checklist of those who have spoken ("chirped") is a handy tool.

...one lawyer on our board begins at least two monologues at each meeting with the statement "I'm not that kind of a lawyer, but..." At that point everyone's eyes glaze over and a noticeable pall descends on the meeting for at least ten minutes... — Barbara

---

DANGER: Solo Performances

Avoid solo performances! These come in a variety of forms: The artistic director of a theatre who spends the first hour of each board meeting presenting the latest stage door gossip in a dramatic performance worthy of a Tony award! The chair who talks approximately 95 percent of the meeting time – doing all committee reports and updates from the chair! The executive director afraid to take a breath for fear a board member will ask an unanswerable question!

VII. ACTING

Axiom 7
The brain can only absorb what the backside can endure!

Some board meetings are notorious for their length and lack of action. Each board meeting reaches the point of diminishing returns – that moment where continuing the meeting becomes more harmful than productive. When a newly elected board Chair decided to end monthly board meetings after one hour (even in mid-sentence if need be), members were suddenly on time, attendance was up and at the end of the year, the board was surprised at how much more productive it had been.

Have you ever heard anyone complain that a board meeting was too short?

Try this

Many well-run boards make a policy of starting on time and include time allotments for each item on the agenda. While these should not be slavishly adhered to, they can signal to board members the relative importance of agenda items.

As a surgeon, I stand for a living – I literally have a hard time sitting for over one hour – 90 minutes tops!

— Brenda

VIII. ENJOYING

Axiom 8
Board service can be fun, interesting and exciting.

Nonprofit board service is a unique part of America's tradition. Citizens voluntarily serve on boards to oversee all aspects of the life of our communities. To retain these dedicated volunteers we call board members, nonprofit boards have to see that board service is an enjoyable experience.

Many organizations forget that their board members are volunteers. All the issues related to motivating direct-service volunteers apply to board members as well. Board members want to:

- Feel that they are contributing.
- See things moving forward.
- Enjoy the time they spend in service to the organization.

...my experience on this board has been exhilarating and exasperating, but overall it has been fun. I have met people I would never have met, testified at a congressional hearing, presented our mission to the CEO of my corporation and done things I would never have had the opportunity to do if I did not agree to serve on this board. All this – and the satisfaction that I helped the organization achieve its mission of helping troubled teens stay in school! — George

Try this

Celebrate the awarding of contracts or the successful completion of a special event by spending some time at the meeting reviewing the organization's accomplishments. Take pictures at events – and share them as the board members arrive.

* * * *

Putting It Together

Making full board and board committee meetings work successfully is a real challenge. Two overriding themes can be the glue that holds all the planning, working, learning, deciding, connecting, speaking, acting, and enjoying together.

Commitment

The motivating factor for board members is their commitment to the mission of the organization. A group of board members providing governance oversight of an organization is ultimately successful when it is transparent to each board member that the task at hand – fundraising, strategic planning, purchasing capital equipment, public relations campaigns – furthers the mission of the organization.

Humor

People are funny, a group of board members around a boardroom table can be funnier! While striving for efficient and effective meetings, we would do well to remember that even at the most critical moments of an organization's life, we are fallible people who are capable of the most sublime wisdom and the most ridiculous failures!

Some meetings produce more than others – and sometimes meltdown occurs. Commitment with a strong dose of humor helps us deal with both scenarios.

David Michael LaGreca

David LaGreca is a man with a past. He has done it all. He is a teddy bear of a man with a marvelous sense of humor, clarity and vision and a backbone.

David has been a Program Director at Volunteer Consulting Group since 1991. His responsibilities include board recruitment and consulting, board training, the corporate placement program, VCG's national initiatives and overall management of VCG's information systems.

Prior to joining VCG, David was the Administrator for the Department of Surgery, Memorial Sloan Kettering Cancer Center.

He also taught at Boston College, wrote a newspaper column in Rhode Island and has spent the last fifteen years working with community based health care organizations caring for terminal patients.

A graduate of the Katholieke Universiteit te Leuven, Belgium, he received his MBA from the Columbia University School of Business. As a former diocesan priest and Jesuit novice, David worked with a wide variety of nonprofits which address issues covering education, health care, homelessness and human rights. He has served as a volunteer, staff and board member.

A native of Rhode Island, David has lived, worked and studied in Belgium, England, Germany, Italy, Jamaica and Tanzania. He can order a meal just about anywhere.

He served as Chair of the Board of *Body Positive of NYC* (1993-1997) which provides services to HIV infected and affected men and women; he has also served as a Body Positive trainer and group facilitator.

David M. LaGreca
Volunteer Consulting Group
6 East 39th Street
New York, New York 10016-0112
1-800-291-2364
dlagreca@vcg.org
www.vcg.org

Don't take a chance
when it comes to planning.

CHAPTER 5

Mission-Based Strategic Planning: The Key to Your Organization's Survival

Terrie Temkin, Ph.D.

There's an old saying that if you don't make dust, you eat dust! Unfortunately, too many nonprofits plod along, doing business as usual, relying on what they perceive as their importance to the community to keep them afloat. Dan Austin, a professor at Nova Southeastern University, put it this way: "Just because you are on the side of angels doesn't mean you are going to survive." Mission-based strategic planning can make the difference between life and death for organizations in this rapidly changing world.

AN INTRODUCTION TO STRATEGIC PLANNING

The concept of strategic planning means different things to different people. According to J.M. Bryson, author of *Strategic Planning for Public and Nonprofit Organizations,* it is "merely a way of helping key decision-makers think and act strategically." It can be geared toward the short term – often referred to as operational planning – or long term. It can be done by a single staff member or involve wide representation from the staff, board, and community. Typically, it includes a look at trends; a review of the mission; the development of a vision; the establishment of goals, as well as the design of action steps to ensure achievement of the vision and mission; and the institution of ongoing evaluation. Contingency planning is a key element of strategic planning.

When nonprofits commit to "strategic planning," they are generally referring to a process by which stakeholders in the organization give many hours over a period of several months to set the organization's direction for the next three to five years. The specific objectives of this process are to:

- Assess the external environment within which the organization operates to determine trends that will affect the organization.

- Evaluate the organization's position in the marketplace.

- Reevaluate the organization's mission in light of the trends and the organization's position.

- Put the organization's values into words that all understand and buy.

- Set an organizational vision that provides direction and stimulates forward thinking throughout the organization.

- Determine the type and degree of organizational growth expected over the next three to five years.

- Evaluate the strengths and weaknesses of the organization.

- Determine how to capitalize on the strengths and minimize the weaknesses to achieve the organizational vision.

- Determine the long-term applicability of the organization's current programs in light of the trends and vision.

- Determine specific goals, new programs, priorities and action plans for the coming year.

- Determine general goals, new programs and priorities for the next three to five years.

- Determine how the organization will commit its resources over the next three to five years.

- Establish criteria for assessing the organization's success in meeting its plan.

Why is strategic planning necessary? First and foremost, it provides direction, ensuring that the organization is working toward its mission. After all, that is the reason for the organization's existence. All too many organizations today tend to use a shotgun approach. They hear of an interesting program or grant opportunity and go after it without considering whether – given their particular mission – it is the best application of their limited resources. Strategic planning is also valuable because:

- It keeps the organization on the cutting edge.

- It suggests the most effective and efficient ways of preparing for the future.

- It provides a common vision for everyone involved in the organization.

- It encourages buy-in.

- It allows for continuity as people move in and out of the organization.

- It spells out what the organization expects of everyone involved.

- It allows the organization to make the most of its resources.

- It communicates a sense of organizational stability to the community.

- It minimizes surprises that could be disastrous to the organization.

- It encourages contingency thinking throughout the organization.

- It is often required by funders.

- It helps keep the organization in business.

The physicist Tom Hirshfield once said, "If you don't ask, 'Why this?' often enough, somebody will ask, 'Why you?'"

PLANNING TO PLAN

A meaningful plan will result only if everyone involved understands the commitment he or she is making and what that commitment means in relation to other organizational responsibilities. Therefore, organizations looking to do strategic planning should begin by answering a series of questions.

- What is your purpose in undertaking this process? The commitment of organizational resources may differ depending on your response.

- Are you committed to the process? Are you willing to invest the necessary time, effort and money?

- Who is to be involved in the process? Have you considered representatives from all stakeholder groups? Have you included individuals from all levels of the organization?

- Where will the planning meetings be held?

- How long will the meetings last?

- What time is best to hold these meetings? Will you use one or more weekend retreats? Will you devote a portion of each board meeting to the process or will you set dedicated meetings?

- What materials will the committee members need prior to each meeting?

- What kind of audiovisual equipment is necessary? It may be as simple as a flip chart, marker and tape or as sophisticated as an electronic meeting system.

- Who will collect, copy and distribute the materials?

- Who will lead the process? Will it be someone from inside the organization or an outside facilitator?

- If it is an outside facilitator, will that person be required to participate in the entire process or will his or her involvement be limited?

- Who will serve as a liaison between the facilitator and the board, staff and community members?

- Who will handle the clerical work that comes out of this process?

- Who outside the organization should be included on the planning committee?
- How will the results of the plan be communicated?

THE PROCESS
Assessing the Trends

Assuming that the answers to the above questions lead to the decision to undertake formal strategic planning, I suggest starting with a look at the trends. As the World Future Society suggests, "Knowing the possibilities of the future – that is, what *might* happen – enables people to choose... to make the desired possibilities become realities and prevent the undesired possibilities from ever being realized."

In assessing trends, it is critical that you look not only at both internal and external factors that may impact your organization, but also at how people view your organization in relation to these factors. Key factors that deserve your attention include:

Internal	External
Mission	Government
Vision	Economy
Organizational values	Funding sources
Programs	Community needs
Services	Clients (both current and potential)
Organizational hierarchy	Consumer values
Control issues	Privatization
Staffing needs/resources	Opportunities for collaboration
Space needs/utilization	Social trends
Equipment needs	Demographics
Efficiency levels	Volunteers
Marketing needs/resources	Accrediting bodies
Budget	Technology
Evaluation methodologies	Competing nonprofits

There are a number of techniques you might use to complete the trend-analysis process. The first is simply to codify the information you already know. For instance, you may have noticed that the last three grant proposals required the demonstration of some collaborative effort with another agency. You could draw the conclusion that funders will increasingly seek projects that demonstrate such collaboration.

The second is to research the trends that others have identified. Futurists regularly publish books (for example, the *Megatrends* series, by John Naisbitt and Patricia Aburdene, and *The Popcorn Report* by Faith Popcorn), in magazines (such as, *The Futurist,* published by The World Future Society), and on the Internet (see, for instance, http://208.201.254.94, a project of InfoWorld Futures). Daily newspapers and the government documents section of the public library are rich sources of information about trends, as are professional associations and watchdog organizations. The Points of Light Foundation, Independent Sector and the National Center for Nonprofit Boards are just three professional organizations that regularly publish trends in the nonprofit sector. The Independent Sector, along with OMB Watch, keeps track of legislation with the potential to influence the sector.

The third technique is to survey people who would have the information you need. For instance, you might gather information from colleagues, competitors, clients, legislators, or staff people working out in the field. You can post questions about trends on a computer bulletin board or invite someone active on a number of community boards to share his or her perspective with your group. You can also conduct focus groups, written surveys or one-on-one interviews with key informants.

Fourth is using the technique of scenario building. This is where your own creative thinkers hypothesize what the world might look like in three to five years. Generally, a number of scenarios are generated, based on different factors that might significantly impact the organization. For instance, the group might consider what the world at large and the organization in particular might look like if technology continues to explode at its current rate or all public support should disappear.

Case studies are also useful for trend analysis. By looking at actual situations faced by organizations similar to your own, you can draw conclusions about those activities that may be most productive and those most likely to be counter-productive.

Simulation games can be used to anticipate the future. Some experiential activities, such as Maxis' *Sim City 2000* (and now, *Sim City 3000*), require participants to make decisions with potentially far-reaching consequences based on a set of variables of which they may or may not be aware at the time they make their decisions.

Finally, you may turn to computer calculations to assess probable outcomes in situations that can be quantified. For instance, you can determine the likely financial situation of your organization should your membership significantly increase or decrease or should your foundation funding dry up.

When assessing the potential validity of a forecast, futurist Andy Hines suggests you evaluate several factors. Among them:

- Does the forecaster's credentials or reputation suggest specialized knowledge in this area?

- Is he or she relatively free from any bias that could skew the forecast?

- Are the assumptions upon which the forecast is based valid?

- Are there markers against which the forecast can be tracked for accuracy?

- Does it appear that the forecast is missing any critical piece that could affect the conclusions that have been drawn?

- Do the conclusions seem logical based on the steps the forecaster used to reach them?

Once you have determined the trends and the likelihood of their accuracy, it is important to determine what they mean for your organization, your clients and your community. Will you be required to move your offices, modify your staffing patterns, or change your programming focus to stay current with community needs? Would it be advisable to rewrite your policies? Frances Hesselbein, president and chief executive of the Drucker Foundation, states that defining the implications of trends is the essence of strategy.

As many people as possible should be involved in gathering and analyzing the trends. Besides giving people a unified big picture, involvement increases buy-in for the broader strategic-planning process. The organization benefits from a diversity of perspectives and contacts. Having more people involved also means having more people to do research or conduct interviews.

Identifying Core Values

Once you have identified the trends, it is important to ask the stakeholders about the role they feel the organization can play in the expected new world order. This is a multifaceted question that leads to the mission, vision and goals that ultimately give the organization its strategic direction. However, the underpinnings of that question are the core values in which the stakeholders believe, the core values that propel everyone into action.

As individuals, we understand how values such as honesty and reliability guide our everyday actions. Ken Blanchard and Michael O'Connor, authors of *Managing by Values,* believe values guide the everyday actions of organizations as well. If, for instance, an organization believes that everyone has a right to a safe environment and to respect from others, that organization will set its priorities and make its decisions with those principles in mind. Of course, there must be agreement among stakeholders about what values will guide the organization.

Reevaluating the Mission Statement

The mission statement defines the raison d'être of your organization. It should be based on the core values and drive every decision your organization makes.

Obviously, as the world is changing around your organization, the mission may be affected. Therefore, the strategic-planning process should include a reevaluation of the current mission statement.

Reevaluation is particularly critical when:

- The need addressed by the mission no longer exists.

- The need addressed by the mission is no longer relevant.

- The need addressed by the mission is no longer compelling or motivating.

- The people working for the mission are unclear about it.

- The organization is not producing mission-related outcomes.

- More and more resources are being funneled to projects not directly related to the mission.

- The support for your mission no longer exists.

- You see the need to expand the scope of the mission.

- Others in the community are working toward a similar mission.

- You begin to collaborate with other organizations in the community, so your role must be refined or redesigned.

- The environment changes significantly.

- A number of years have passed without evaluation of the mission.

If your evaluation indicates the need or desirability for a change in the organization's mission, your earlier assessment of the trends will point up specific ways in which the content should change. A new mission statement must be more than simply appropriate, given the tenor of the times, however. It must be clear. It should succinctly explain – in language that is free from organizational jargon – what your organization does, for whom it does it, and how the organization differs from others appearing to address similar needs.

Nonprofit management guru Peter Drucker cautions, "Less is more applies to most mission statements. If they run more than a paragraph, they haven't been thought through." The idea is that the mission statement reflects the organization's big picture. It should not be too specific because it must remain broad enough that your organization can work with it in different ways as the needs and the climate change. However, because the mission should drive all organizational decisions, it must be specific enough that it provides focus.

Setting an Organizational Vision

A vision statement draws a picture of what the world will look like once the organization reaches its mission. For instance, an organization may seek to end hunger in its community (the mission). Its vision might be to create a world where people have sufficient job training to find and keep jobs that pay a living wage and where food giveaways in esteem-affirming settings are a daily reality for those who still would fall between the cracks.

Walt Disney was fond of saying, "If you can dream it, you can do it!" The vision statement is the dream that drives the organization's activities. Properly communicated, it is highly motivational.

An easy way to identify your organization's vision statement is to ask key stakeholders, "If you were to turn on 'Good Morning America' three years hence, and this organization were being honored, what accomplishments would the hosts be recognizing?"

Remind the stakeholders to consider in their answer the trends, the organization's mission, its customers, and the values of both the organization and its customers, as well as the elements of an effective vision statement. Those elements, as identified by Burt Nanus in *Visionary Leadership,* are:

- It is future-oriented.

- It is likely to lead to a better future for the organization and the community.

- It is appropriate for the organization – that is, it fits the organization's history and culture.

- It reflects the organization's values.

- It sets standards of excellence.

- It clarifies the organization's purpose and direction.

- It inspires enthusiasm and commitment.

- It reflects the uniqueness of the organization.

- It is ambitious.

Setting Goals

In Lewis Carroll's *Through the Looking Glass,* Alice is in Wonderland and finds herself at a fork in the road. Confused about which direction to take, she happens to look up into the tree situated at the edge of the road. Staring down at her is the Cheshire Cat. Alice asks the cat which road she should take, and he asks where she is headed. Alice replies that she doesn't know. The Cheshire Cat tells her simply, "Then any road will take you there." The mission, vision, and values provide a destination for the organization. Goals, broken down into specific action steps, serve as the road map detailing how the organization can reach that destination.

Goals are the outcomes you wish to achieve, specified in measurable terms wherever possible. For instance, if your vision includes being financially stable, you might state goals such as having nine months-worth of operating expenses in reserve by the end of the next fiscal year and achieving within five years an endowment fund that generates $100,000 in annual interest. The criteria against which you can measure the organization's success are clear with outcomes stated in this way.

Initially, different committees might be charged with generating a list of outcomes reflective of their unique perspective of what it would take to achieve the organization's mission and vision. However, eventually these individual lists have to be merged and ranked in importance. The criteria against which specific goals should be measured include the degree to which they are mission-oriented, critical, realistic and necessary for the achievement of other critical goals.

Designing Action Plans

Once the group has prioritized the goals, it is time to determine the action steps it will take to accomplish them. This means considering such factors as staffing needs, time requirements, prerequisite conditions, equipment, and indicators of success. It also means looking at how best to maximize those factors that can enhance your ability to accomplish the organization's goals, as well as how best to minimize the impact of those factors that may inhibit goal achievement. **(See Figure 1.)**

Figure 1
PLANNING FOR GOAL ACHIEVEMENT

	GOAL		
FACTORS PROMOTING ACHIEVEMENT		FACTORS INHIBITING ACHIEVEMENT	
FACTOR	ENHANCE THIS FACTOR BY...	FACTOR	LIMIT EFFECT OF THIS FACTOR BY...

Adapted from Kurt Lewin's Force Field Analysis.

Let's go back to our goal of creating an endowment fund that generates $100,000 in annual interest. The action steps might include:

- Combating the fear that gifts to the endowment fund will take away from current funding needs.

- Writing a policy that diverts to the endowment fund 10 percent of all unrestricted contributions.

- Forming an investment committee composed of a lawyer, stockbroker, trust officer, accountant, and major gifts solicitor.

- Exploring and settling on investment options.

- Determining how to market an endowment fund, as it is rarely as compelling as current program needs.

- Writing and printing brochures to promote the new fund.

- Hiring a part-time planned-giving officer who would also staff the endowment.

- Increasing the budget by $50,000 to pay for the new staff member.

- Setting appointments with each of the $5,000-and-up contributors to begin to cultivate awareness for the need for gifts directed to the endowment fund.

To ensure that the steps are well-thought out and that there is buy-in from those that will be charged with carrying them out, the action steps typically are determined in committee. Depending on the goals, it may be appropriate to form new standing or ad hoc committees.

The committees might codify their plans on a planning chart. **(See Figure 2.)** By detailing the order of the action steps, the time frame in which each step should be accomplished and the responsible individual(s), there is a written record to serve as both implementation guide and commitment to action.

Figure 2
PLANNING CHART

OBJECTIVE	PRIORITY	CRITERIA FOR SUCCESS	ACTION STEPS	TARGET DATES (EACH STEP)	INDIVIDUALS RESPONSIBLE	PROGRESS REPORTS	COMPLETION DATE

Setting goals and action steps are the tasks in the strategic-planning process that tend to excite the stakeholders most. In fact, there will be individuals who will try to jump in at every planning meeting with ideas of how to improve the functioning of the organization. However, as the *Through the Looking Glass* parable suggests, it is critical to hold people to working through the process in an orderly fashion.

Evaluation

All too many organizations invest tremendous human and financial resources in a strategic plan, then put it on a shelf. Evaluation, along with goal modification, must be an integral part of the strategic-planning process.

While a tickler file with the projected completion dates of each action step is one way of evaluating the progress being made toward the organization's goals, it is helpful to do a formal review of the entire plan at least twice a year. The purpose is to determine whether the organization is achieving the results to which it committed. And if not, why not?

Questions to ask in an evaluation include:

- Are the targeted results still desirable? If not, what targets are more desirable, and why?

- Are the selected methodologies still the most appropriate way to implement the goals? Or, given your experience, do you believe another approach would be more beneficial?

- Is the organization's progress creating any unexpected complications that must be dealt with?

- Is the plan coming in within budget? If not, are the perceived benefits worth the additional expenditures required?

- How are the stakeholders and the members of the general community responding to the changes?

- Should you continue your program of action or shift gears and apply your resources elsewhere?

Expect that modifications to your plan will be required. As the world continues to change, so will the needs of your organization. Planning is an ongoing process. In the words of an unknown "philosopher": "When the going gets easy, it's time for a reality check.....you might be going downhill!"

TECHNIQUES FOR IMPLEMENTING THE PROCESS
Soliciting Input

We all know the adage that two heads are better than one. Whether your group is discussing trends, values, a mission statement, the organizational vision, or goal selection and prioritization, individuals must have a way to offer their perceptions and recommendations to the group.

Brainstorming

Though it's been around forever, brainstorming is still an extremely effective method for soliciting input from a group. Everyone knows the basic procedures:

- The group generates as many ideas as it can, while a recorder jots them down – generally on newsprint that is then hung around the room for all to see and refer to.

- Judgment is kept out of the process until all ideas have been put forth.

- People are urged to piggyback on others' ideas and to be creative in their responses. After all, if the same-old, same-old worked, the organization wouldn't be searching for something different.

To maximize the options the group generates, wait until everyone agrees there are no more ideas to give, then insist that the group come up with at least 20 more. The group may complain that the goal is impossible. However, the ideas originating from this point forward are often the strongest because they come from outside the proverbial box.

The Crawford Slip Method (Modified)

Another technique for soliciting input is the Crawford Slip Method. This method ensures that everyone has an opportunity to voice his or her ideas. A small group might begin by determining the issues the organization needs to explore. A list of questions is then designed around these issues. The questions must be open-ended and free of implied answers. For instance, instead of asking for the marketing needs of the organization, the group might ask for the general needs of the organization.

Everyone is given a stack of evenly cut pieces of bond paper, 3 x 5 cards, or Post-It Notes. Information gathering begins when people are asked to generate their responses to each question on the slips – putting only one self-contained, comprehensive idea on each. If an idea requires explanation or contains several parts, the additional information is recorded on new slips. Dr. Claude Crawford suggested that people all write in the same direction and avoid abbreviations and symbols to aid in the interpretation and organization of the slips.

The slips are collected and shuffled without regard to the questions they answer. A few people are asked to categorize them on a large table or on the wall. Initially, the slips are laid out randomly. As general themes emerge, items are put into piles and the piles are labeled using a title card of a different color or size. Simple but specific key words should be used on the title cards. Then, so that each stack can be found quickly, the stacks are alphabetized.

Once each slip has been categorized, the piles can be manipulated into an outline format that speaks to the relationship between and within the piles. If necessary, individual slips can be moved from one category to another based on the logic that is emerging.

While the process may have to be repeated to explore certain issues in greater detail, what the group ends up with is an ordered list of recommendations for an effective intervention. For instance, it may decide that staffing issues are the first to be resolved and that, within this category, all job descriptions must be rewritten before the organizational chart can be revised or new people hired.

Building Agreement

At each point in the planning process, it is important that people reach some degree of accord, or there will be no buy-in when it comes time to implement the plan. Yes, it is usually difficult and time-consuming to get everyone to agree on anything. However, there are a number of techniques that give everyone a voice and result in quick, adequate decisions. Among them are straw-vote cards, colored dots, the decision matrix and multi-voting.

Regardless of the technique you choose, begin by reminding the group of your purpose and any directives, such as trends, values, mission or vision, that they have already identified. Ask whether any of the items require clarification, and whether any items are similar enough that they can be collapsed into one another. This will prevent split votes and speed the process.

Straw-vote Cards

Select card stock in two colors. For this process, red for *stop* or *no* and green for *go ahead* or *yes* are very appropriate. Give everyone a card in each color. As each option is read, ask people to hold up the card that best describes how they feel about that option.

Agreement is suggested by an overwhelming show of a single color. A fair mix of both colors suggests the need for additional discussion.

Colored Dots

Write out the various options the group is considering, and post them around the room on the walls. Give everyone colored coding labels, such as those made by Avery. Generally, the process works best if people receive enough dots to vote for 20 - 25 percent of the options proposed.

Ask people to read the proposed items and to put one or more dots by their favorites. You'll find the dots tend to cluster around items, making it vividly apparent which ones the group likes best.

This technique is fast and fun. It may be varied by giving people dots in different colors and asking them to prioritize their choices according to color.

Decision Matrix

Create a matrix displaying suggested goals on the vertical axis and names of decision-makers on the horizontal axis. Give everyone a set number of points to place on the matrix according to their perception of priority. For example, if each person is given 100 points, one person might assign all 100 to a single item. Another might divide the 100 points among all the items equally. Yet another might assign 60 to one item, 30 to a second, and 10 to a third.

After everyone has assigned his or her points, compute the average for each item. Those with the highest totals become the priorities. (See **Figure 3**.)

Figure 3
DECISION MATRIX

	Mary Smith	John Carne	Scot Day	Sally Flower	Total
Design and implement capital campaign	15	20	30	30	24
Increase number of volunteers by 20%	5	10	10	15	10
Begin collaboration with local nonprofits to share office space	60	35	30	40	(41)
Centralize all operations	20	35	30	15	25

Multi-voting

Faced with a long list of options? Ask people to select those they would rank in the top third of the list (that is, if there are 27 items, they may select nine). A show of hands as each item is read allows a quick tally of the votes.

Eliminate those items that received the fewest votes. Then, begin the process again, limiting the choices to the top third of the now-reduced number of options. Repeat each step until the list has been reduced to a manageable number and reveals a clear ranking.

Whichever technique you use, some stakeholders will walk away feeling that they, or their priorities, are unappreciated. Minimize the negative impact of this reality by setting the stage before any voting takes place.

Give people a chance to clarify anything that is unclear. Remind them to look at the big picture when doing their ranking – to consider the organization's agenda before their own. Suggest they ask themselves: What identified needs – if satisfied – would bring the organization closest to accomplishing its mission? What potential solutions would have the greatest long-term impact? How will each item under consideration affect the budget?

One Last Word About Process

If you try to finalize every aspect of the process in the large group, you will never complete the plan. Have the group identify its top two or three choices, then select a small ad hoc committee to wordsmith and bring the final result back to the group for approval.

CONCLUSION

Thomas Carlyle once said, "There is nothing more terrible than activity without insight." In today's world, where funders are demanding accountability and competition is forcing organizations to change or close their doors, nonprofits must know exactly why and how they are undertaking each activity. Strategic planning that is mission-based provides not only the insights but also the direction that keeps organizations viable.

BIBLIOGRAPHY

Barry, Bryan W. 1986. *Strategic Planning Workbook for Nonprofit Organizations.* St. Paul, Minn.: Amherst H. Wilder Foundation.

Blanchard, Ken, and O'Connor, Michael. 1997. *Managing by Values.* San Francisco: Berrett-Koehler Publishers.

Bryson, John M. 1995. *Strategic Planning for Public and Nonprofit Organizations.* San Francisco: Jossey-Bass Publishers.

Eadie, Douglas C. 1995 Putting vision to powerful use in your organization. *Nonprofit World,* 13(4), 40-45.

Hesselbein, Frances. Winter 1998. Journey to transformation. *Leader to Leader,* (7), 6-7.

Hines, Andy. 1996. A checklist for evaluating forecasts. In Edward Cornish (Ed.). *Exploring Your Future: Living, Learning, and Working in the Information Age* (pp. 82-86). Bethesda, Md.: World Future Society.

Howe, Fisher. 1997. *The Board Member's Guide to Strategic Planning.* San Francisco: Jossey-Bass Publishers.

Lewis, C. Patrick. 1997. *Building a Shared Vision: A Leader's Guide to Aligning the Organization.* Portland, Ore.: Productivity Press.

Long-range Planning Manual for Board Members. 1993. Akron, Iowa: Aspen Publisher, Inc.

Maxis, Inc. *SimCity 3000* (http://www.store.ea.com)

Migliore, R. Henry; Stevens, Robert E.; Loudon, David L.; and Williamson, Stan. 1995. *Strategic Planning for Not-for-Profit Organizations.* Binghamton, N. Y.: The Haworth Press, Inc.

Naisbitt, John and Aburdene, Patricia. 1990. *Megatrends 2000: Ten New Directions for the 1990's.* New York: William & Morrow, Co. Inc.

Nanus, Burt. 1992. *Visionary Leadership.* San Francisco: Jossey-Bass Publishers.

Popcorn, Faith. 1991. *The Popcorn Report.* New York: Doubleday.

Rice, James J. 1997. Strategic visioning in non-profit organizations: Providing a clear direction for the future. *The Journal of Volunteer Administration* 15(4), 30-39.

Scholtes, Peter R. 1995. *The Team Handbook* (23rd printing). Madison, Wis.: Joiner Associates, Inc.

Terrie Temkin

Terrie Temkin is a perfectionist. It's apparent in everything she touches, from her elegant style of dress to tweaking a time line for a strategic plan. An award-winning speaker and an engaging group facilitator, she brings 25 years of nonprofit management and adult education experience to her work.

Author of a biweekly column in the Miami, Herald entitled "On the Board," Terrie is also editor of *Nonprofit Management Solutions* – a quarterly newsletter. She has written and presented numerous papers, her articles being found in such publications as Advancing Philanthropy, Board Member, Community Jobs, Nonprofit World and many more. She is currently working on a book for the National Center for Nonprofit Boards on choosing a consultant.

For 9 1/2 years, Terrie served as executive director of the largest, most creative and financially productive district of Women's American ORT, a national organization that supports a worldwide network of vocation schools. Prior to that she served as a special events fund raiser for the American Heart Association, a program director for the Wisconsin Region of the B'nai B'brith Youth Organization and a nationally recognized trainer for Hospital Learning Centers.

Despite a busy consulting practice, Terrie finds time to volunteer. She served on the board of the Business and Professional Women's Network of the South Broward Jewish Federation. She is in her third year on the Ft. Lauderdale board of the American Cancer Society and was appointed to the Forward Community Resources Coordination Council and the Florida Education and Employment Council for Women and Girls.

Terrie Temkin, Ph.D.
Nonprofit Management Solutions, Inc.
P.O. Box 7536
Hollywood, Florida 33081
954 985-9489 • Fax: 954 989-3442
Temkin@polaris.acast. nova.edu

CHAPTER 6

Structuring Your Board to Achieve Maximum Results, or Which Comes First the Chicken or the Egg?

Mike Schroeder

The chicken or the egg, the cart or the horse, the structure of the board or the work of the organization. When defining what is most important to a new or restructuring not-for-profit, the fine lines between chickens and eggs, carts and horses can be even more obscure. This is especially true if the organization's primary visionaries are unwilling to make tough decisions about whether the content of the work to be done ought to dictate board structure, or whether the structure needs to be in place before decisions are made about what is important to the organization.

The traditional model of not-for-profit management argues that an appropriate structure of standing committees should be in place before the organization considers the work these bodies undertake. In such a model, the board would most frequently include an executive committee – probably made up of the board chair, the secretary and treasurer, and the chairs of each of the standing committees, a group that might include the finance, nominations, resource development, public relations and program committees. While this model, with some variation, has successfully served the not-for-profit community for decades, I suggest we have an opportunity, in this age of tremendous competition and change, to take another look at our options. For those of you just beginning your work in this field, the cart and horse should be clearly within your view; for others, I suggest we take a step back, widen our perspective for a few moments and consider what is essential to our organizations.

In their 1996 article for the *Harvard Business Review* titled, "The New Work of the Nonprofit Board," Barbara Taylor, Richard Chiat and Thomas Holland reached a number of powerful conclusions based on twelve years of research into what makes effective boards work and what hinders ineffective boards. After observing dozens of boards at work, having conversations with hundreds of board members across the country and developing a survey to measure board success and board members' satisfaction, here is what they learned about how board members view their service:

1) "The work of the board is trivial, insubstantial and perceived by board members as unrelated to organizational success or failure.

2) "Meetings are boring, scripted and ritualized, with little opportunity to influence unresolved matters, and board members are given too much information and too little perspective on strategic issues and outcomes.

3) "Boards consistently underperform."

For anyone involved with non-profit management, the study is a wake-up call to pay attention to our board members and to perhaps redefine the work done by this most important and essential group. These are the Michael Jordans of our organizations. Imagine your board members suddenly deciding to take a sabbatical from your organization, ala Jordan's decision several years ago to leave his team – the Chicago Bulls – to try his luck with baseball. After a season during which they struggled mightily, the Bulls were fortunate enough to regain Jordan's interest and his services, thanks to untold dollars worth of contractual enticements and a commitment from the coach, Phil Jackson, to make basketball – Jordan's work – interesting again. Most of us can't afford to ply our board members with financial enticements, so let's focus on our opportunity to make the work more interesting and meaningful.

Consider that board members are committed to the organization and want it to be successful both in the short and long terms. To extend the sports analogy, board members want to be on a winning team that contends for championships. That desire can be broken down into five basic elements. Think of these items as contract demands made by your board members. They want:

1) A voice in deciding what's important to the long-term future of the team.

2) To hear from the coach – the organization's chief executive – what's important.

3) To really know how the team is performing and be involved in devising measurement tools used to determine success.

4) An atmosphere accepting of change.

5) An opportunity to be role models for the rest of the team.

Giving your star players what they want may require rethinking the board's very nature and structure. The first step in such a process is for the board to assume a position of partnership with management in determining issues central to the organization's success. Imagine Jordan and Jackson in consultation about what it takes for the Bulls to win the championship. The board works in cooperation with the chief executive in identifying strategic issues and then develops a board and organizational agenda that is focused on issues that can have a real impact on the organization.

Finding out what matters to an organization involves the following four activities by board members:

1) Asking key questions of the CEO – getting the big picture – and guiding the collaborative effort to formulate answers.

2) Risk becoming vulnerable – that is, accessible and accountable – and get to know the organization's key stakeholders.

3) Get educated on the important information regarding the organization's industry. Consult experts.

4) Decide how success is defined. Board and management should determine a top 10 list of critical indicators of success and use these vital indicators to assess the organization's overall condition and to identify potential problem areas.

Once the core issues have been agreed upon – decision-making that will lay the foundation for a strategic plan – the substance of the work to be done for the year should dictate the structure of committees and meetings. Committees, work groups and task forces must mirror the institution's strategic priorities. That may seem self-evident, but too often boards are organized according to function and with little regard for the essential work at hand. Board members are left to deal with low-stakes operational issues. To engage board members in work that really matters, substance must dictate structure. The frequency, format and duration of meetings should be appropriate to the work to be done. The board chair and the chief executive should consider, before each gathering of the board, the meeting's purpose and goals in addition to devising some means for judging performance. Rather than traditional, report-oriented meetings, the board may consider:

1) Moderated discussions in which no vote is taken. The focus here can be on big issues, and such sessions may be opportunities for all members of the board to offer input.

2) Small group sessions that allow board members the opportunity to brainstorm apart from the committee structure.

3) Thematic meetings focusing on a single subject of great importance, such as a change in CEO or a capital campaign.

Ironically, focusing the board on doing work most important to the organization may require new rules of engagement and certainly requires expanding the board's work past its customary role of scrutinizing management. This work has four basic characteristics:

1) It is concerned with do-or-die issues.

2) It is driven by results that are linked to specific timetables.

3) It has clear measures of success.

4) It requires the engagement of the organization's internal and external constituencies.

Of course, boards can't change overnight. Nor should they. Change in this case may involve members rethinking their responsibilities and work schedule. Allowing time for productive discussions and meaningful reporting requires longer, less frequent meetings. Focusing on what matters to an organization may require a redesign of committee structure and an abandonment of standing committees in favor of strategic task forces focusing on specific issues and with clear deadlines. Such task forces disband after the work is complete.

There are times during a board's life cycle when it may be natural to discuss changing board structure and process: a change in leadership, a change in chief executive, a crisis, challenges from constituent groups. Such events should be embraced by board members as opportunities to add more value to the work they are doing. The results may be twofold: measurable success for the organization and an increase in satisfaction for board members themselves.

SIZE OF THE BOARD

Once the substance of the board's work has been decided, it is, indeed, necessary to consider structure. Begin with the legal requirements for boards in the state of incorporation. Some states mandate at least three board members, some two. Determining the right size for an organization's board involves finding a tightrope walker's balance between being small enough to be effective and large enough to achieve desired diversity in points of view.

Small boards can be effective. An active, committed board of seven can often be productive and efficient. And, if the individuals are chosen with specific criteria in mind, seven members may also be enough to represent the full spectrum of constituents served by the organization as well as various points of view. To accomplish all it needs to, an active board of this kind might empower ad hoc committees to consider very specific issues of importance. Such groups can be a tremendous source of information for any board, but particularly for a small one. An ad hoc group – or task force – tends to be disbanded after its mission has been accomplished. A task force might be used to consider a marketing campaign, to decide whether to purchase a building or to set policy in certain areas.

Small boards build a sense of camaraderie and ownership among members. They can be very efficient. The lines of communication are typically well-defined, and members are aware of the key issues. A small board may be augmented by task forces, ad hoc committees or advisory groups that enable the participation of individuals from outside the board.

Some organizations naturally gravitate toward large boards. A national group, for example, may find representation from each state essential. A group that has a very broad constituency may feel compelled to try to have each segment represented at the board level.

Another philosophy – inviting major donors to be board members – can mean large boards. This approach can work. The individuals who make the largest philanthropic donations are most frequently those closest to the organization. They probably feel a real sense of kinship with the mission. Often, however, donors of impact gifts don't want to be involved with the broad issues faced by the board, and they lose interest. In fact, inviting a donor to be a board member without doing an assessment of his or her interests may create a situation with much negative potential. A different, but very real problem arises when a board member/donor attempts to buy influence.

Large boards typically have an active and powerful executive committee, and this is a special challenge. This smaller group may become isolated within the board structure, an island unto itself. If this happens, it is more a fault of the structure than of the individuals involved. The smaller executive committee is typically easier to gather, to communicate within and to build consensus from. This group may very well have a good grasp of the issues important to the organization. The chief executive may find it difficult to form relationships with the larger board and so focuses on the members of the smaller executive committee. This group may meet more frequently than the board itself, and those meetings may be quite efficient.

The danger inherent in this structure is twofold: First, general board members may view themselves as mere advisers to the inner circle that really wields the power and quit offering input. Second,

too often the executive committee makes all the important decisions and expects the rest of the board to comply. The work of the
board cannot be accomplished by a powerful inner circle.

Don't be afraid to ask the question of whether you could function better with a smaller board. If the answer is yes, put the issue
on the table.

If there are good reasons to justify a board of more than 19,
then it is crucial to structure the large board so that everyone feels
meaningfully involved.

There are, of course, weaknesses in working with a board
that is too small. Board size may be dictated by tradition or by an
old boys' or girls' network that resists bringing new people into
the fold. Small boards may lack diversity in background and experience and may limit your organization when it comes to address-
ing critical issues. Burnout may become an issue when too few are
expected to do too much. This may be the case when a small board
doesn't empower task forces or ad hoc committees to assist in
policy-making.

In the end, there is no magic formula for optimum size of the
board. Study the best practices of organizations similar in scope,
survey current leadership on the issue, and consider that the size of
the board may change, depending on your organization's stage in
its life cycle. Don't automatically accept historical decisions on board
size. Remember to organize around what matters to the organization. This is a complicated question and requires an honest and
careful assessment of the situation.

STRUCTURING THE BOARD

Structure is one of the key elements of success for any board.
Without proper structure, board members may become discour-
aged and feel as though the time they spend working on your behalf
is unproductive. Board structure is actually an easy thing to create,
maintain and repair as necessary.

The basic structure of the board should be clearly outlined in the bylaws of the organization. The bylaws should be changed whenever a majority of board members feel there is a more productive means of managing the board's work. Whatever the decision regarding structure, it is important to have buy-in from the organization's leadership. Only then will they make it work.

Here is my top 10 list of suggestions regarding basic structure:

1) Avoid keeping an ineffective structure simply because it's always been that way. Evaluate your structure every couple of years and change it if a majority of board members favor a change. Tradition has its place, but not when it impedes productivity and board members' satisfaction.

2) Keep efficiency in mind when considering board size. There are models of large organizations who effectively govern themselves with small boards, no executive committee and few standing committees. Do your homework.

3) Evaluate everyone, including the chair, as part of the board evaluation or nominating process. This process must be an open one dedicated to finding the best group-process leader on the board.

4) Limit the authority of the executive committee in the bylaws to actions that are necessary between full board meetings. Given the power to do so, an executive committee may gravitate to doing the work of the board, and the board members left out of the decision-making may lose interest.

5) Don't allow the volunteer chairman to act as the chief executive in an organization that has paid staff.

6) All board business should flow through the chief executive, no matter where it originates. Designate the chief executive as the only agent of the board.

7) Limit the number of standing committees. Consider the work that is essential to the organization and form committees, ad hoc groups and advisory bodies around that work. Do not focus on program when forming committees.

8) Find ways to get input from service consumers. Ad hoc task forces can achieve such special functions. Empower ad hoc task forces to consider all alternatives before making recommendations to the board.

9) Consider the formation of an advisory group. Such groups can be effective, lending credibility, visibility and expertise to the organization. Members should have set terms with no term limits.

10) Limit board membership to volunteers. The potential for conflict of interest is great when staff members become board members. Staff members serve as liaisons to the board.

EFFECTIVE COMMITTEES

Committees are one way a board organizes itself to accomplish its work. Although some boards have no committees, most find it productive to have a few.

Here are a few simple questions to ask when considering the setup of committees:

1) Are they necessary, or can the full board deal with all the work itself?

2) If we need standing committees, which ones are appropriate for us now?

3) Should bylaws be changed to reflect decisions regarding committees? The board should have the broad ability to authorize the creation of committees and task forces as it sees fit, within the context of the bylaws. Can policy statements – standard operating procedures – effectively address the details of committee structure? In that case, policies suffice to serve as effective management guidelines for committees.

To the question of which committees, the typical lineup is executive, nominating, finance, resource development and, perhaps, program. Remember to keep the number and focus directly tied to the essential work of the organization. Also, an organization's committee structure may change during different stages of its life-span.

The board should be allowed to appoint committee members who may not be members of the board. This allows it to gain expertise beyond the realm of the board and to involve people whose focus, at least for the time being, may be strictly limited to one specific issue. You may find that this process helps identify new board members, providing both parties an opportunity to audition the other.

Committee chairs should be good managers of people and process. They must be committed to communication with the staff liaison (if one exists) and the board chair. Beware of making this an honorary position.

Matching board members with the organization's committee needs is most often the task of the board chair working in cooperation with the chief executive. Conducting a self-assessment of board members' personal interests and professional experience can help decipher the sometimes mysterious process of mapping out committee assignments. The nominating committee may also be involved with this process.

The general role of standing committees is to draft changes to standing policies and present them to the board for adoption. A committee may also serve as a sounding board for the staff liaison. If it provides advice to staff, it should not be the only source of advice. A committee speaks to the board and not for the board.

Some organizations may be large enough to assign a staff member as a liaison to each committee. Typically, this is a person whose job within the organization fits the role of the committee. The staff liaison then assists the committee chair with preparing agendas, maintaining good communications and preparing minutes. In small organizations, the chief executive may staff all or most committees. At no time does any committee speak for the full board, and policy implementation is best left in the hands of the chief executive, who may then decide to delegate to other staff.

The executive committee has tremendous potential to help, or to hinder, good governance. Executive committees typically exist on boards with more than 15 members. Their role may be to discuss critical issues and then make a recommendation to the board. At their best, these committees offer an expedient process for assisting the full board and staff in making crucial and timely decisions. At their worst, they can become a refuge, often unintentional, for power brokerage and isolation from the organization's constituency and other board members.

A board should include in its bylaws some limits on the authority of the executive committee. This body should not, for example, be able to amend the bylaws, hire or fire the chief executive or elect officers. With the right job description, this committee can be a powerful tool of a fully involved board.

Committees are a structural tool meant to assist the board in achieving its work. The structure of the board should mirror the organization's strategic priorities, with a premium on flexibility and ad hoc arrangements. Committees should not become mini-boards with their own authority, but because of their specialized focus, they can help educate fellow board members and make savvy recommendations for board policy. Used meaningfully, committee assignments can add to a board member's enjoyment of service.

SUMMARY

Taking action to do new work takes work, but it is an opportunity for a board to live its role as model for the organization. If the board is willing to question its mission, structure and method of operation, then the organization as a whole will be willing to do the same. As boards demand evidence of productivity, efficiency and measurable outcomes, they should be willing to model the behavior they seek in others. This process may demand that board members get out of their comfort zones and experience work in areas outside what they know best. Once accomplished, they may find that their effort has inspired them to be more than simply overseers of the administration or suits with deep pockets. Most importantly, they may find the path to more rewarding involvement.

Don't change simply for the sake of change. Consider whether change will help your organization more effectively achieve its mission. If your current structure works, don't abandon it overnight. Try one small change, and keep it if it works. There is no right or wrong way to structure a board or its work; it's a matter of function or dysfunction. The most important elements are to be aware of what you're doing and to monitor your efforts and their outcomes. Change can be made in increments. Continual self-evaluation is essential.

The ultimate goal of any activity of this kind is to create a structure better able to serve the consumers of your service. Measure the value of your management initiatives by that yardstick. Keep your customers foremost in mind.

HOW TO TELL IF IT'S NOT WORKING

- Dead board members still get meeting notices.
- Board members don't come to meetings.
- General board members refer all the tough issues to the executive committee for action.
- Agendas aren't prepared or followed.
- There is no follow-up on action items.
- Board members are unwilling to recruit new members.
- Committees don't meet.
- The mission is not getting accomplished.

Sources

Chait, Richard P., Holland, Thomas P., Taylor, Barbara E., "The New Work of the Nonprofit Board," *Harvard Business Review*, September-October 1996.

Mike Schroeder

If Steven Spielberg ever decides to do "The Mike Schroeder Story," his first call will be to Tim Robbins to play the lead. They share the same tall, athletic build and ready smile. Mike smiles a lot these days as the Vice President for Development for Special Olympics Missouri.

Throughout his career, Mike has managed to combine his three loves – athletics, nonprofit management and journalism. His days as an athlete have been compromised by back problems secondary to the onset of middle age, but he still enjoys writing both fiction and nonfiction.

Mike began his career as editor of "The Viking Report," a weekly magazine about the Minnesota Vikings. He was a reporter for the *St. Cloud Daily Times*, then the Sports Information Director at St. Cloud State in St. Cloud, Minnesota.

He then served as Public Relations Director for USA Hockey in Colorado Springs, Colorado. (He was a hoops man and stayed off the ice except for cocktail hour.) During this period, he was also Editor for American Hockey Magazine. Eventually, he was promoted to Director of Fund-raising for USA Hockey.

In 1993, Mike moved to St. Louis, where he started the St. Louis Vipers, a professional in-line hockey team. It was a for-profit venture that ended with very little profit, but he had great seats to the games.

Mike joined the Special Olympics Missouri staff in 1995, first as the St. Louis Metro Director, then as Vice President for Development.

Early in the days of his 15-year nonprofit career, Mike found himself in a late-night smoke-filled committee meeting when a fistfight broke out between committee members. Things have changed a lot in the past 15 years. Mike no longer allows smoking!

Mike Schroeder
6175 Kingsbury
St. Louis, Missouri 63112
Phone: 314-721-6064 • FAX: 314-721-3669

CHAPTER 7

Legal Issues: Reducing Risks of Personal Liability

Donald W. Kramer

Nonprofit board members often worry about being sued.

It's one thing to give their time and attention – and even some money – to a good cause. It's quite another to risk unlimited personal liability if something goes wrong.

Although relatively few nonprofit board members have actually been sued for their conduct as board members – and far fewer have ultimately been found liable for damages – their concern about potential personal liability is real and pervasive.

Organizations that want to attract and keep good board members take pains to be sure that the board members' personal exposure is reduced. Changes in state and federal laws in the last decade and an increasing sophistication in purchasing insurance have given nonprofits a greater ability to provide protection for their board members and their organizations.

But the ultimate responsibility lies with the board members themselves – to show up at meetings, pay attention, ask "impertinent" questions, act in good faith, and use their best judgment in pursuit of the mission of the organization.

Board members are properly concerned about two kinds of liability.

First is potential liability to unrelated third parties for injury or property damage arising from their acts or omissions on behalf of the organization. This type of "tort" liability is substantially the same as they face in their daily activities, where they can be sued for negligent driving that causes an auto accident, for example, or negligence in leaving a banana peel on the floor that causes a guest to slip and fall during a cocktail party.

Second is the potential for liability to the organization and its members for failing to fulfill their "fiduciary" duties. These include the duty of care, to exercise good faith and reasonable judgment in making business decisions, and the duty of loyalty, to avoid putting their own interests ahead of the interests of the organization.

Most nonprofit organizations are corporations (and not trusts, unincorporated associations or other types of entities). The board members may be called directors, trustees, members of council, managers or some other name. By whatever name, the members of the governing body of the organization are responsible for the business and affairs of the corporation.

Limitation on Personal Liability

One of the great benefits of the corporate form is its limitation on personal liability. Normally, an individual is not personally liable for a breach of contract or other improper conduct of the organization itself, or for that of other employees or agents of the corporation. The protection does not apply, however, to the personal conduct of the individual. Every individual is responsible for his or her own actions.

A board member of a nursing home would not ordinarily be personally liable, for example, if a nurse's aide dropped a resident while trying to transfer the resident to a wheelchair.

Although the home might be liable for the negligence of the aide, its employee, the board members would not be personally liable for the aide's conduct.

If, however, the board had specifically decided not to train the nurse's aides in how to make such transfers, knowing that the failure to train created a risk of harm for the residents, a member of the board who had agreed with that decision might be personally liable for the resident's injury.

The classic case of personal responsibility was illustrated by a suit involving a California condominium association in the mid 1980s. A resident complained that the outside lighting was inadequate to deter someone from breaking into her first-floor unit. The board decided not to increase the lighting. When the woman added her own lights, the board turned off her lights and the previously existing lights as well. An intruder broke into the woman's unit and assaulted her.

When the woman sued, the court said that the board members could be sued personally because they had affirmatively decided to shut off the lights and the injury was a foreseeable consequence of that decision.

(A board member who disagrees with a decision such as this should be sure that the minutes of the board meeting record the disagreement and the negative vote. A dissenting board member should not be personally liable if the decision later proves to have been a bad one and the board members who made it are sued.)

Whether a board member is ultimately held personally liable for an injury in a case such as this may depend on the standard by which the board member's conduct is measured. And the standard may depend on whether or not the board member is a volunteer for the organization.

Volunteer Protection Acts

During the 1980s and early 1990s, most states passed volunteer protection laws (sometimes called "shield laws") to reduce the likelihood of personal liability for volunteers for charitable organizations. Some laws provide complete immunity from suit except in cases of gross negligence or intentional injury. Some, such as Pennsylvania's, provide that a volunteer will not be held personally liable unless the volunteer's conduct falls "substantially below" the standard of conduct of "similar persons" "in like circumstances."

These laws were originally passed in reaction to a series of suits against volunteer coaches of children's sports leagues. The laws were intended primarily to protect direct-service volunteers and to remove what was perceived as a barrier to their participation in the programs. The protection is not limited to participants in the direct work of the organization, however. It applies to the work of volunteer board members as well.

In 1997, Congress passed the federal Volunteer Protection Act shortly after the Presidents' Volunteer Summit in Philadelphia. This federal law provides that volunteers for charities and certain other civic groups will not be personally liable for their acts or omissions if they are acting within the scope of their responsibility for the organization and the harm is "not caused by willful or criminal misconduct, gross negligence, reckless misconduct, or a conscious, flagrant indifference to the rights or safety of others."

The statute also provides that a volunteer will not be liable for punitive damages even in cases of gross negligence or recklessness. The federal act is effective in all states unless a state passes a law within three years to specifically opt out of coverage.

The federal law, like most state laws, does not protect the volunteer from liability for injuries caused by the operation of a motor vehicle. Also like most state laws, it does not relieve the organization itself from liability for the negligent or improper acts of its volunteers.

How do board members get protection from potential liability? First, the board members will want to consider whether they should be paid for their services. Because of the protective statutes, a volunteer is less likely to be personally liable than a paid participant. Most board members of charities are volunteers. Reimbursement for expenses incurred in performing volunteer duties ordinarily does not count as compensation or cause a board member to lose volunteer status. (A volunteer who itemizes deductions on a federal income tax return and does not accept reimbursement for out-of-pocket expenses may deduct the costs as a charitable contribution.)

The most significant form of protection, however, comes from liability insurance. Board members are almost always included as named insureds under general and professional liability policies maintained by nonprofits. It is important, however, to consult with an experienced broker to be sure that the board members are named and that the policies provide adequate coverage. Even if the board members have not acted improperly, the insurance will provide their legal defense. If the cost of paying the defense lawyer is the personal responsibility of the board member, that amount alone, even without ultimate liability for damages, could be ruinous.

Fiduciary Duties

The second area of potential liability for a board member is breach of fiduciary duty to the organization itself. A board member who gets an unreasonable and undisclosed fee on a business transaction with the corporation, for example, would clearly fall into this category and would violate the duty of loyalty. Allowing large amounts of cash to be left for long periods in non-interest-bearing checking accounts, rather than being invested for the benefit of the organization, might violate the duty of care.

Duty of Loyalty

The "duty of loyalty" is pretty clear. The board member may not put his or her interests ahead of the interests of the corporation. The most obvious areas of danger involve economic conflicts of interest. Some boards take the position that they will have no financial dealings with any member of the board. Most, however, are not absolute so long as the conflict is disclosed before the transaction is entered into, the deal is fair to the corporation, and the arrangement is approved by a majority of disinterested members of the board.

Because so many charities are dependent upon public support through contributions or volunteer effort to pursue their mission, the public disclosure of improper private benefit to an insider can substantially undermine the credibility of the organization and cripple its program. The question of impropriety, even when the conduct is entirely disclosed and entirely legal, can cause problems when portrayed in an unfavorable light by an investigating reporter. In extreme cases, insider scandals have hurt the credibility of the entire nonprofit sector.

Nonprofits should develop conflict policies that, at the least, require the disclosure of any potential conflict and the approval of any transaction by a disinterested majority of the board.

This issue is even more important now because Congress has given the Internal Revenue Service the power to impose an "excess benefits" tax under the "intermediate sanctions" provisions added to Section 4958 of the Tax Code in 1996. The IRS may impose a tax on a "disqualified person" who gets a benefit from the charity in excess of the value of the goods or services he or she provides in return. A "disqualified person" includes a board member and any other person in a position to exercise substantial influence over the affairs of the corporation.

The statute was passed primarily to curb unreasonable compensation for executives, but it is broad enough to cover any arrangement with a disqualified person. An excessive fee for a professional service from a board member, payment for a spouse to travel with a board member to the national convention, or any other economic advantage of any kind might be taxable.

The implementing Regulations proposed by the IRS set elaborate procedures for obtaining data on comparable transactions, which will give the organization a "rebuttable presumption" that the transaction is fair.

(Board members of private foundations are under an even greater restriction against "self-dealing" in almost all business transactions other than payment of reasonable compensation for services.)

Duty of Care

The "duty of care" is usually spelled out in the state nonprofit corporation law. Although the exact wording may vary from state to state, these statutes generally provide that a board member has a duty to act in good faith, in a manner the board member reasonably believes to be in the best interests of the organization, and with such care, including reasonable inquiry, skill and diligence, as a person of ordinary prudence would use under similar circumstances.

Each of these phrases, of course, could be the subject of litigation, but the statute usually gives guidance on some of them.

Many statutes provide, for example, that a board member may rely in good faith on information presented by officers or employees of the corporation, by counsel, public accountants or other professionals, and by committees of the board, so long as the board member reasonably believes them to be reliable and competent. A board member will not be acting in good faith if he or she relies on a report with knowledge that the reliance is not warranted.

Some statutes provide that, in considering the best interests of the corporation, a board member may also consider the effects of any action on "any and all groups," including employees, suppliers and customers of the corporation, and the communities in which it operates. Provisions like these were also added in the 1980s as a reaction to business corporate takeovers and stockholder suits seeking to have board members consider solely the maximum price for a takeover bid.

Some statutes further provide that, absent a breach of fiduciary duty, lack of good faith or self-dealing, actions will be presumed to be in the best interests of the corporation.

In effect, these statutes have created a slightly expanded "business judgment rule," which has traditionally protected board members from personal liability where their actions have been reasonable and in good faith. Courts have been reluctant to impose personal liability on board members merely because a decision turns out to have been a bad one, so long as they acted reasonably in making the decision in the first place.

Some of the newer statutes on board members' liability go even further to protect a board member from personal liability. The Pennsylvania statute, for example, provides that the corporation may enact a bylaw that provides that a board member shall not be personally liable for actions taken as a board member unless the board member has breached the fiduciary duty spelled out in the statute and the breach constitutes self-dealing, willful misconduct or recklessness.

Under this provision, mere inattention would not result in personal liability unless it was reckless inattention. The protection of many of these laws does not apply to breach of criminal statutes or liability for the payment of taxes.

(The one area in which nonprofit board members can legitimately lose sleep at night is the organization's failure to pay over federal – and sometimes state – payroll withholding taxes. A person "responsible" for those payments may be personally liable if they are not made. Court cases make clear that mere knowledge that others are being paid when withholding the taxes are not being turned over may enough to create responsibility and personal liability. It is natural to want to pay the loyal staff and continue the program even when the money gets tight. But financing those operations with withholding taxes is a huge personal risk.)

Is Limited Liability a Good Policy?

Is it really good public policy to say that a board member is not personally liable if he or she fails to pay attention to what is going on and lets the corporation stumble into a substantial problem? Wouldn't the world be better off if board members had a greater duty to be careful?

Theoretically, the answer is probably "yes." But as a practical matter, many nonprofits seeking individuals to give of their time and talent for a charitable mission have found that the prospects are reluctant to risk their personal assets. Many potential board members want to be sure that they have the maximum protection and the minimum risk if they are going to join the effort.

Most state legislatures have recognized this and enacted the protections to increase the pool of talent available for the voluntary sector.

Board Members Are Entitled to Protection

What happens if a board member is sued for injury to a third party for an alleged breach of fiduciary duty? The board member looks to the corporation for "indemnification" against personal loss, for protection for the payment of attorneys' fees and other costs of suit, amounts for settlement, and, in many cases, even payment of adverse judgments.

Indemnification rights are also largely created by state statutes. Although the language may vary from state to state, several concepts usually apply.

Indemnification is not limited to board members or to volunteers. Paid personnel and other representatives of the corporation are also eligible for the protection. Indemnification usually applies to investigations or other "proceedings" – civil, criminal and administrative – whether pending or "threatened" and is not limited to actual litigation. It usually covers claims against the board member in his or her capacity as a representative of the organization.

The corporation is usually *required* to indemnify a board member who is "successful" in defending against a claim.

The statutes permit voluntary indemnification in many other cases, such as those in which the board member settles the claim and, in certain situations, even where the board member may be found liable. Indemnification can usually cover settlements and often fines and judgments. Normally, to be entitled to indemnification, the board member must have acted in good faith and in a manner he or she reasonably believes to be in the interests of the corporation. Under the Pennsylvania law, indemnification is not permitted if the board member's conduct constitutes willful misconduct or recklessness.

There is also usually a prohibition on indemnification where the board member has been found liable to the corporation itself for breach of duty in a so-called "derivative suit" on behalf of the corporation. If a board member has to pay money back to the corporation because of the board member's improper conduct, it makes no sense for the corporation to give the money to the board member to pay the claim back to the corporation.

Most statutes provide that no indemnification may be made until a determination has been met in each case that the board member meets the qualifications for indemnification. The determination must usually be made by a quorum of board members who are not involved in the proceeding or, where such a quorum is unavailable, by an independent attorney.

Finally, corporations are usually allowed to advance the costs of legal defense where it appears that the board member meets the qualifications for indemnification and the board member provides a commitment to repay the money if it is ultimately determined that the board member is not entitled to it.

To some extent, these obligations and rights are included in the state statute of the state of incorporation. Savvy board members, however, will want to see specific provisions granting them the maximum protection included either in the articles (or certificate) of incorporation or in the bylaws of the organization. These documents act as a form of contract between the corporation and the individual board member and provide greater assurance of protection.

Protect Board Members Through Insurance

How does a nonprofit back up its promise to indemnify? Unless it has substantial assets of its own, to be meaningful, the answer is probably insurance. General and professional liability insurance usually covers bodily injury or property damage to other people. Directors and officers ("D & O") insurance provides protection against claims of breach of fiduciary duty and other types of wrongful acts.

(Board members may be covered under plans maintained by their employers or under their own "umbrella" policies maintained for excess coverage under their personal homeowners or automobile policies. The nonprofit board, however, should do what it can to provide adequate protection through the organization.)

With D & O insurance, a number of important issues should be considered.

D & O insurance was traditionally written to provide two areas of coverage. It covered the individual board members and officers and, subject to certain exclusions, would pay their litigation defense costs and settlements or judgments if they were sued on a claim. It also reimbursed the corporation to the extent that the corporation advanced such payments.

Traditionally missing from the coverage was protection for the organization itself for the wrongful acts of its representatives. With the expansion of volunteer protection acts and director liability laws, it is certainly possible, even likely, that an individual would not be personally liable for an action but that the corporation would be liable for the results of the action.

The president of the board might not be personally liable, for example, for a discriminatory termination of the executive director if the president's actions were not willful misconduct or recklessness. But the corporation could still be liable for the wrongful conduct of its officer.

Most modern policies now cover the organization itself, and nonprofits should be sure to maintain such coverage.

Nonprofits must also be careful about the exclusions in the policy. Insurance companies do not want to cover the costs of a grudge match when one faction of the board sues another faction over a matter of "principle." Most policies, therefore, contain some form of "insured versus insured" exclusion, denying coverage when one person who is named as an insured person under the policy sues another person who is also a named insured.

The nonprofit wants to provide protection for as broad a group of individuals as possible and wants to be sure that present, former, and future board members, as well as members of committees and other volunteers are included among the named insured where possible. But these individuals are also the most likely to start a suit because they are the ones who care the most about the organization. Without proper tailoring of the exclusion language, the protection of the policy can be substantially undercut by expansive coverage of individuals.

Nonprofits must beware of attempts to exclude coverage of employment disputes, which create the largest single category of claims under D & O policies. This is an important coverage to maintain, including protection against claims of discrimination, wrongful termination and other charges.

The organization will also want to assure that the policy advances the costs of legal defense before the final outcome of the litigation or proceeding. With the expense of litigation today, it may be impossible for an individual to carry the burden of defense costs personally to the conclusion of the case.

Finally, the corporation will want to be sure that non-monetary claims are also covered by the policy. If someone sues for access to financial books and records, for example, the policy should cover the defense of that claim if it is opposed by the board.

As with any insurance, the nonprofit should work with a knowledgeable broker who can appropriately advise on the amount and scope of coverage. D & O insurance has become more available in recent years, and can usually be obtained at reasonable rates, perhaps between $1,000 and $3,000 for the average small or midsized nonprofit. If an experienced broker is not readily available locally, a national or state association of similar nonprofit organizations can usually help find knowledgeable brokers and appropriate plans.

Insurance is invoked only when there is a problem. If the coverage is not right, or is not sufficient, it's too late to change it after the claim is filed.

Board Risk Management

Beyond insurance, how do board members protect themselves from potential liability? By affirmatively running a strong program in pursuit of the mission of the organization.

The object of serving on a nonprofit board is not to avoid liability. The object is to advance the mission of the organization and probably, in some way, to make the world a better place in which to live.

That requires proactive measures, not defensive tactics. The likelihood of doing the job is enhanced with a diverse board of individuals who are not afraid to ask "dumb questions," who actively present different points of view, who remember the reason they are there, and are willing to act.

William G. Bowen, former president of Princeton University and the Andrew W. Mellon Foundation and author of the 1994 book *Inside the Boardroom: Governance by Board Members and Trustees*, has concluded that "courage and the will to act are often the attributes in scarcest supply" on a board. "In my experience," he says, "after some amount of time and discussion . . . it usually becomes fairly clear what should be done. The trick is marshaling the energy – and especially the courage – to act."

Considered action is not likely to lead to personal liability. It *is* likely to lead to successful programming that allows a nonprofit to do what it is supposed to do. The board member's role is to make that happen.

Don Kramer

Don Kramer had to make a decision whether to pursue a career in journalism or law. After attending Princeton University and Harvard University Law School, he found he could effect change most effectively doing both.

Don has more than 30 years of experience dealing with the concerns of nonprofit organizations; a lawyer, teacher, writer, publisher and board member. He has worked with nonprofits of all types and sizes, helping structure start-up situations and restructure multi-organizational health and educational systems. He counsels on a wide range of corporate, tax, real estate, charitable giving and other nonprofit issues.

He is the editor and publisher of *Don Kramer's Nonprofit Issues,* a national newsletter of "Nonprofit Law You Need to Know." He lectures frequently on nonprofit issues, and teaches a course on "Legal and Government Issues Affecting Nonprofit Organizations" in the masters program in nonprofit management at Eastern College.

Don currently serves as a member of the Board of Directors of the Pennsylvania Association of Nonprofit Organizations. He is a member of the advisory boards of La Salle University's Nonprofit Management Development Center and the masters program in nonprofit management at Eastern College.

When not writing, volunteering or practicing law, Don enjoys canoeing and running.

Don Kramer
Montgomery, McCracken, Walker & Rhoads, LLP
123 S. Broad Street
Philadelphia, PA 19109
215-772-7277 • Fax: 215-772-7620
E-mail: dkramer@mmwr.com

For a free copy of *Don Kramer's Nonprofit Issues,*
call 1-888-NP-Issue, or request through the web site at
www.nonprofitissues.com.

CHAPTER 8

Building a Strong Board – Executive Director Relationship

Fern E. Koch

There are strong boards and there are weak boards. Strong boards promote a power-sharing relationship between themselves and their executive directors. They go through orientations and training and learn the differences between policy and operations. They support their chief executives, do their work in committees and insist on being properly informed before making decisions. Weak boards, on the other hand, neglect policy, interfere with operations and micromanage their executive directors. They are made up of friends and cronies of the executive director or the board chair. Often these are people who don't even bother to come to meetings. In organizations with weak boards, board members and chief executives alike become frustrated, angry or bored. Before you accept a board position, try to find out if you are about to serve on a strong board or a weak one. If you already serve on a board, follow the seven principles below to help build a stronger, more effective board of directors – one on which you will be proud to serve.

Promote a Power-sharing Relationship Between the Executive Director and the Board

The ideal board-staff structure can be described as power-sharing. Boards take care of governance, and paid staff take care of day-to-day operations. Peter Drucker, one of the world's most stimulating management thinkers of our time, believes the board and the executive director need to work together as a "team of equals."

Robert D. Herman and Richard E. Heimovics, authors of *Executive Leadership in Nonprofit Organizations* and long recognized for their work in nonprofit research, call the ideal structure "shared leadership." They stress that the executive director needs certain "board-centered leadership" skills to produce the ideal working relationship.

The National Center for Nonprofit Boards, which was established *"to improve the effectiveness of the nation's nonprofit organizations by strengthening the capacities of their leadership,"* has several publications that promote the theory that governing boards need to develop "a new style of leadership, one that is shared between staffs and boards" or "a new and more balanced relationship and a sharing of power and authority." Cyril Houle, author of *Governing Boards*, refers to this shared responsibility as a "board-executive system of dual authority."

A successful nonprofit organization embraces a power-sharing structure and strives to have both an effective board and an effective chief executive. Even though there is no doubt that the executive is the employee and the board the employer, the board and executive director need to work together as a team – each responsible for separate and distinct parts of running the organization. The board establishes and monitors policy. The administration, headed by the executive director, implements policy. The separation of duties and responsibilities is important to the structure and must be maintained.

In the nonprofit arena, the head of the operational arm is usually referred to as the executive director although other titles may be used including chief executive officer, or CEO, and chief professional officer, or CPO. They all refer to the top paid administrator of the organization.

The division of responsibility in any nonprofit organization generally follows functional lines. The question should be asked: Is a specific task a board function or staff function? This does not mean that every issue is either a policy function or an operational function. The line between policy and operations does not run straight, down the center. Often it zigs and zags from one side to the other. There are many fuzzy areas which need to be worked out among the executive director, the board and the chair.

The board's job of governance should be reflected on its structure chart. This is the first step in creating a working relationship between the board and the chief executive. Because the board is responsible for the failure or success of the organization, board members cannot and should not relinquish their power and authority to anyone, not even their chief executive officer. They cannot legally transfer their responsibility.

The executive director is employed by the board of directors and has operational, or the day-to-day, responsibilities while the board has policy-making responsibilities. Together they share the leadership of the nonprofit organization.

Board Members and Executive Directors Need Orientation and Training

Neither the quality of the board nor the quality of the chief executive officer can be left to chance. Orientation and training must be provided for both.

Board development is often neglected in the nonprofit arena. For some reason, we think that the minute the election is over, everyone instinctively knows exactly what to do to be an effective board member. Obviously, this does not happen. There is no magic wand.

The goal is not to have a strong board and a weak executive director or vice versa. The goal is to have both an effective chief executive and an effective board working together as a team of equal participants toward a common goal – to fulfill the mission of the organization. Together they provide the basis for a successful organization.

Through orientation, board members become familiar with the organization they are about to serve. With ongoing training, board members learn about their duties and responsibilities, legal liabilities and how to make policy decisions.

One of the best tools board members can have during their term of office is a good board manual. A three-ring binder is ideal because as the organization grows and changes, so can the board manual. A board member's manual includes such items as the agency's mission and vision statements; the bylaws and articles of incorporation; financial information including copies of the latest audit, annual report, current budget and information about the

Contents of an Orientation Manual

Mission/Vision Statements
Goals and Objectives
Organizational Fact Sheet
Bylaws
Structure Chart
Long Range Plan
Board Plan of Work for Year
Most Recent Budget
Most Recent Audit
Most Recent Annual Report
Most Recent Financial Report
Investment/Endowment Information
List of Major Donors
Organization's Policies
Agency Newsletters/Brochures
Minutes of Last Six Board Meeting
Descriptions of Programs/Services
List of Board Members
Staff Roster
Board Member Job Description
Solicitation Letter
List of Committees with Charges
Executive Director's Resume/Job Description

funding sources plus a list of investments or contracts; policies including the personnel policies; program descriptions and copies of brochures; board member and executive director job descriptions; the strategic plan and plan of work for the year which would list meeting dates and locations as well as important events or fundraisers; minutes from the past four to six board meetings, board and staff rosters; copies of recent newsletters and other publications; a summary of the directors and officer's liability insurance and a solicitation letter, along with a response envelope.

In many agencies, orientation manuals are distributed to new board members at a meeting where they meet the staff and fellow board members. At such a meeting, they might hear about the history of the organization, tour the facilities and learn about the fundraising activities and the services provided by the agency.

Board development is not a luxury, it is a necessity. Having basic information about an organization in a single orientation manual, board members are more prepared to participate in critical decision making. In many organizations, orientation is not even a consideration. New board members are left on their own to find the answers to their questions. They are expected to help make decisions in a vacuum, with very limited background and knowledge. In some organizations, orientation consists of a packet of information, lunch with the executive and a tour of the facility. If board members are untrained, how can they be expected to do an effective job? If we don't look at how individual members perform while on a board, how can we know if they have developed into a quality board. Board performance directly relates to organizational effectiveness.

Clearly, when board members have not been trained, they do not know what they are supposed to do or not do. They do not know the difference between policy work and administrative or operational work – between governance issues and management issues. When board members have not received orientation and training, they tend to become frustrated and confused about their roles. They are likely to get bored, disgruntled, cause dissention or even drop off the board.

It is critical that board development be given serious attention. Too often, organizations pick "any warm body" – anyone willing to join the board, without regard to the quality of service. Often organizations spend time selecting and recruiting the very best people to serve only to have them fend for themselves – to figure out what it is we want them to do. The truth is, board development begins with "the ask." Board member responsibilities and expectations should be discussed with the person upfront – <u>before</u> he or she accepts the nomination. After the election, a thorough and more formal orientation and training should take place.

It is a good idea for new board members to experience the programs of the organization firsthand. In a local Meals on Wheels unit, for example, orientation requires a two-day commitment from new board members. On the first day, besides listening to presentations and overviews, they actually deliver meals to the homebound seniors. On the second day, they are taken on a tour of the commissary and eat lunch there – the same kind of meal that is being delivered to the elders that day.

Every new board member (and every new executive director) can benefit from a thorough orientation – even those who have served other organizations in similar capacities. Some organizations consider orientation and training so important they include a provision in their bylaws making it a requirement, and some go so far as to outline when it should take place. Unfortunately, too many organizations do it in a haphazard manner or fail to conduct orientation and training at all. Orientation and training are absolute necessities for building strong boards, and strong executive directors.

The Board's Job is Governance

Many executive directors report that board members interfere with operations while unknowingly neglecting their policy responsibilities. Many board members misunderstand the meaning and importance of policy. The textbook *Business Policy Text and Cases* contains a definition of policy that perfectly fits the nonprofit model and addresses many questions regarding the work of governing boards.

It says, "*policy is the study of the functions and responsibilities of senior management, the crucial problems that affect success in the total enterprise, and the decisions that determine the direction of the organization, shape its future, and when well implemented, secure its achievement.*"

Policy says what needs to be done, and administration or operations carries it out. The chief executive can be instrumental in helping the board set policy as well as in helping distinguish between policy and operational tasks. The executive can and should play a major role in making board experiences as challenging and rewarding as possible.

In the nonprofit setting, policy focuses on the functions and responsibilities of both the executive director and the board. It also reflects a division of responsibility that has to be worked out for each organization's board-executive relationship. It includes not only the development of such things as the strategic plan, organizational goals and objectives, policies, job descriptions, and bylaws but also policy implementation, evaluation and ongoing monitoring of performance. Policy also includes the work of the nominating committee in keeping the board supplied with new and skilled people who will help them fulfill the mission of the organization.

Policy addresses the crucial problems that affect the success or failure of the organization. Besides the obvious financial matters, it also includes issues related to programs or services; membership, if it applies; public relations or image; facilities or property management; and both paid and volunteer personnel. Finances involve not only the expenditure of funds but banking and investment policies and the preparation, approval and monitoring of budgets. It includes fund-development aspects, such as determining how much money is needed, how it will be raised – and by when. What will an organization do or not do to raise money? Will your organization run an event that involves questionable moral values, such as nudity, gambling, smoking or sexual promiscuity? Should an organization that serves children accept a gift of stock in a liquor or a tobacco company? A Girl Scout Council, for example, once struggled with the decision of whether or not to accept cigarette company stock.

Will any and all donations be accepted – even those with strings attached. One organization was faced with the decision of whether or not to accept a building that was willed to it. Not only was the building in need of extensive renovation, but it also had historic preservation status. A year later, the group was still struggling with the complicated issues of securing the many certificates and permits needed to move ahead.

Decisions that determine the direction of the organization or the shape of its future are policy decisions. To illustrate: Many years ago, part of the mission of the American Lung Association focused on eradicating tuberculosis. Portable x-ray units were brought into neighborhoods. Citizens had their chests x-rayed free of charge, in an effort to detect and treat tuberculosis. When it was determined to be no longer a public health threat, the board of the Lung Association changed its mission to include antismoking and clean-air issues.

Policy also involves the ongoing monitoring of plans as they are being implemented to ensure that the goals are achieved. Plans can easily stray off track and inadvertently change direction.

The concept that governing boards make policy and executive directors carry out the policies is simple but the implementation of this division is harder than it sounds. There are many gray areas.

Many executive directors, for example, feel that board members dump work on them. Often, board members, in taking on a committee task, fail to follow through on assignments and instead have staff members perform their duties. This can be a real problem if there is a small staff or if the executive director is the only person on staff and is expected to serve as a resource to ten or fifteen committees. Committees need support services, but it should be made clear from the beginning, what kinds of support are needed and who will provide it. Careful planning and coordination must take place to ensure that everyone works as a team. The division of responsibility has to be worked out among all parties involved and written down so that misunderstandings can be avoided.

Informed Boards Make Informed Decisions

Board members must insist on having full knowledge and open discussion on every issue brought before them. Board members not only expect to be informed but they have the right to be informed. The executive director must provide the board with enough information to allow it to make responsible decisions on behalf of the organization. The executive also helps board members understand their roles and responsibilities and where the line falls between policy-making and administration. In a well-functioning nonprofit organization, the executive takes responsibility for assuring the division of authority functions properly.

Boards Do Their Work in Committees

A common problem recognized by board members and executive directors alike is that many boards do committee work at board meetings. Consequently, board meetings go on for hours. One chief executive complained that, for an hour and a half, her board discussed the color of the carpet in the staff lounge.

In a governing board structure, committees are set up so that work can continue between board meetings. When an issue comes up, the board after initial discussion, may give it to a committee for further study and recommendation. The committee meets, researches the problem, looks at the options and brings forward a recommendation for board action. Committees do not have decision-making powers unless previously granted by the board. The only exception to the rule is the executive committee if such authority has been given in the bylaws. Most states allow for provisions in the bylaws allowing the executive committee to make decision in certain periods on behalf of the board.

In a very real sense, committees are "policy influencers." Through their research and study, they influence how policy will be made. But because the board has overall responsibility for the well-being of the organization and is ultimately liable for everything the organization does, its decision-making power should not be relinquished to anyone – not even a respected committee.

No Surprises

Another important doctrine is one of "no surprises." It requires the chief executive to be candid in sharing the progress, plans, problems and successes of the organization. Likewise, it requires board members to ask questions.

Executive directors who hide problems from their boards or who sugarcoat problems cause more trouble than they bargained for. This kind of attitude can encourage people who should be dealing with administrators to take their grievances directly to the board. The executive who releases the details of a merger with another organization to the papers before her board knows about it is showing a lack of respect for the board's role and authority. One actual board, according to a story on the Internet, found out about a jail sentence for its chief executive when it was published in the newspapers. I suspect the board was more than a bit surprised, but worse, the work of the board was interrupted.

The "no surprises" rule applies to the chief executive and board alike. One chief executive reported that, even though he plans the agenda with the board chair, in the board meetings the chair invariably asks for a detailed report to be presented on the spot with no prior notice. Board members have been known to withhold important information from the CEO, only to have the chief executive surprised and embarrassed when he or she hears it for the first time at a board meeting or in the media. One board member cornered the chair of a local foundation at a Rotary Club meeting and learned that the large grant his organization was counting on went to a competing program. Instead of notifying the chief executive beforehand, the board member announced the bad news at the board meeting, then asked the executive to instantly explain Plan B.

Resist Micromanaging Your Executive Director

If it is difficult to please one boss or one supervisor, it is impossible to please twelve or fifteen or twenty-five. That's the dilemma of the executive director of a nonprofit organization. It is also the dilemma of the board. So how does a board oversee the work of the chief executive? Supervision by 20 or 30 people is difficult to conceptualize, but it can be done. The board supervises the chief executive in five ways.

First, measurable goals and objectives have to be in place, with expectations for the executive director's individual performance clearly defined.

Second, make sure the executive director's job description is accurate and up-to-date.

Third, ensure that the relationship between the chair of the board and the chief executive is healthy and productive. This relationship is critical to the health of the organization and, until recently, has been under-emphasized. Building a good working relationship sets the example for the rest of the organization. Relationship building and communicating are two of the most important ingredients in maintaining a good board-executive partnership. Communication must flow both ways – and take place often – at least once a week but preferably several times a week. It has to be timely, specific and comprehensive.

Fourth, a board should receive regular written reports from the executive director. The reports should include the "**3 P's**": **Progress** made toward reaching the goals of the organization; **Problems** facing the organization; **Plans** for the future as they relate to the goals, progress or upcoming events.

Board members' dissatisfaction with an administrator often comes when they have the sense that the chief executive is withholding information, trying to get away with something or being autocratic. Regular, detailed and written reports not only keep the board informed, but they also serve as a record for the organization and as a reflection of the chief executive's accomplishments. Besides monthly reports, it is also a good idea for the board to receive quarterly or biannual reports, where the 3-P's are described for that period.

The **fifth** and final way a board supervises the executive director is to regularly conduct performance reviews. Even though this responsibility is often defined in the bylaws, it is frequently neglected. From the chief executive's standpoint, a performance review is a way of identifying his or her strengths and weaknesses. It lets the chief executive know what he or she is doing right and what needs correcting. If an organization has a policy that requires performance reviews for staff, it becomes a legal requirement to conduct performance reviews for the chief executive as well.

Five Ways Boards
Supervise
the Executive Director

Measurable Goals and Objectives

Current and Accurate Job Description

Positive and Productive Relationship

Written Reports from the Executive

Annual Performance Review

Good executive directors effectively administer the work of the board. Some underestimate the amount of time and energy it takes. Others fear that the board will micromanage or interfere with operation if it is given too much information. But the truth of the matter is that board administration is an important function of the chief executive officer. The board has a large job to do but it cannot do it without the help and support of the executive director.

We cannot assume that all chief executives know how to work with nonprofit boards – many do not. Herman and Heimovics found, through empirical research, that more than half of all CEOs had no prior experience working with nonprofit boards. With the exception of those whose organizations are part of a national group, many executive directors do not receive executive directors' training; however, this is rapidly changing. Colleges and universities, from Harvard University to local community colleges, are offering nonprofit management courses to help emerging professionals. Still, new executive directors are being left on their own – to figure out what the organization does, how the work is done or even what kind of performance is expected of them. For this reason, orientation and training are just as important for the chief executive as they are for board members.

Executive directors who are founders of the organization for which they now work have added challenges. We can safely assume that they know a great deal about the organization and have the passion and drive to meet the mission, but they often lack the management skills necessary to run a nonprofit organization. In these instances, it is a good idea to evaluate the strengths and weaknesses of the individual and create a professional development plan designed to enhance his or her skills. Management training in such areas as human resource administration, budgeting and finance, grant writing, or project management might be required.

Seven Steps to Building Stronger Boards

Promote a Power-sharing Relationship between the Executive Director and the Board

Board Members and Executive Directors Need Orientation and Training

The Board's Job is Governance

Informed Boards Make Informed Decisions

Boards Do Their Work In Committees

No Surprises

Resist Micromanaging Your Executive Director

Conclusion

The future of your organization depends on the quality of the board. The board is responsible for making sure that it is strong and credible because, in the end, the success or failure of the organization rests in its hands. The only way to improve the quality of the board is to improve the quality of the individuals serving on it. And remember that the goal is not to have a strong board and a weak CEO or vice versa. Instead, you want to have both an effective executive director and an effective board working together as a team of equals toward a common goal – to fulfill the mission of the organization. Together they provide a solid foundation for a successful organization.

Fern E. Koch

When you first meet Fern Koch, you immediately feel at ease with this warm, approachable woman. As you get to know her, her strong organizational skills and talents as a negotiator, trainer and grant writer become apparent.

Fern is a founder of the Nonprofit Management Center (formerly Volunteer Consultants 1979-1993) in Buffalo, New York. She is the Senior Vice President of Marketing and Public Relations. Nonprofit professionals and volunteers flock to attend their yearly conference on nonprofit management at Chautauqua Institution, New York.

Prior to her work at the Nonprofit Management Center, Fern was president of the Girl Scout Council of Buffalo and Erie County; executive director of the Camp Fire Council of Buffalo and Erie County; and Director of Development for Meals on Wheels of Buffalo and Erie County.

Fern is an instructor at Niagara County Community College and the State University of New York, Empire State College where she teaches board governance and fund raising for nonprofit boards of directors, administrators and managers of volunteer programs.

She currently serves as a community volunteer for such organizations as the United Way, Meals on Wheels and the Lupus Foundation.

Fern E. Koch
Nonprofit Management Center
Houghton College at West Seneca
910 Union Road
Buffalo, NY 14224
716-674-2662 or toll free 800-610-6564
Fax: 716-674-2688
E-Mail: FCP@AOL.com

Yuppies change priorities.

CHAPTER 9

People Raising: A New Perspective on Volunteer Resources

Susan J. Ellis

Imagine your reaction if, as a long-time board member, you discovered a part of your organization that you never knew existed. This component involves tens or even hundreds of people and provides services well in excess of what you thought your budget could cover. Besides the value of these services to the clients and the staff, your organization also gains community ambassadors – though you have no idea what they might be saying about you. Would you feel that this component was worth the board's time or attention?

Surprise! You have only to look around your organization to see that you do indeed have this invisible resource working for you right now. These are the volunteers who contribute their energy and skills almost every day, all year long. In your organization, you may call them "members" or "interns" or "auxilians" instead of, or in addition to, "volunteers." Regardless of what you call them, if your board does not involve itself in planning and supporting their work, you are missing an enormous opportunity.

Nonprofit organizations are founded by volunteers, governed by volunteers, and accept the services of millions of volunteers to support their work. But the subject of volunteers is usually neglected in the boardroom. Much of the literature on boardsmanship also ignores this vital area. But this chapter will show how a little board governance goes a long way toward successful volunteer involvement.

In a small organization, the responsibility for involving volunteers may be shared by everyone and therefore "owned" by no one, so the board has the responsibility of assuring oversight. At the other end of the spectrum, you may have a fully-organized and staffed volunteer services office. This does not let the board off the hook. Consider that you may also have a development office, but the board still talks about raising money, right? Well, this is about "raising people."

It's probably occurred to you that board members are volunteers, too. Is there a connection between board volunteers and other volunteers in the organization? Should there be? And keep in mind that *being* a volunteer does not automatically zap you with the knowledge it takes to develop a visionary volunteer program for your organization.

WHY VOLUNTEERS DESERVE THE BOARD'S ATTENTION

Volunteers are a legitimate subject of concern to a board of directors because:

- It is a governance decision to discuss how central volunteers should be to the service delivery of your organization.

- As contributors to your organization, volunteers should be seen as part of any resource development strategy.

- Volunteers are your unpaid personnel department and may even outnumber employees.

- Volunteers have enormous potential in public relations, fundraising, public education, legislative advocacy and other community outreach functions.

- Volunteers are a source of valuable information for planning and evaluation purposes, but only if someone asks for their opinions.

BECOME INFORMED

What do you know about current volunteer involvement? Does the board have concrete information about this human resource just as it has for other areas of the organization's work? Unless you understand the present picture of volunteerism in your organization, it will be hard to formulate vision and policy for the future.

Ask for basic data about volunteers to be included in regular reports to the board. Observe patterns over time. If the numbers or types of volunteers change significantly, ask questions. Be sure you have answers to the following questions:[1]

- Where in our organization do volunteers work? Where do they not work? Why? What activities do they perform?

- How many volunteers are active at any given period in each area of our organization? Are we experiencing difficulties recruiting the volunteers we need? Why?

- What is the demographic profile of our volunteer corps: gender, race, age, education, geography? Was this profile actively sought or did this evolve on its own? Is there enough diversity? Is it what we want?

- What trends and issues are affecting volunteer involvement in our organization?

- How much staff time is devoted to volunteer management?

- What evaluation is being done of volunteer accomplishments, and what are the findings of this evaluation?

If it seems hard to answer these queries, consider it a red flag. Maybe no one knows because not much is being done or no one has been paying attention.

ANSWER KEY QUESTIONS

Whether you are just starting out with a volunteer program or have had one for years, it is never too late (or too early) to lay the proper foundation for volunteer involvement. The following are the major board decision-making areas.

---

1 This chapter is adapted in part from material in "The Boards Role in Effective Volunteer Involvement," by Susan J. Ellis (Washington, D.C.: National Center for Nonprofit Boards, 1995).

Rationale

Why do we want volunteers? This is not an irrelevant or irreverent question! Many nonprofit organizations involve volunteers as though it were self-evident that having volunteers is a good thing for every setting.[2] Or worse, some organizations fall back on volunteers as a reluctant strategy for coping with insufficient funds. Volunteers are tolerated as a "second-choice" arrangement until more money can be raised and the "right" staff hired.

A lack of funds is a poor reason to recruit volunteers. Instead, as a board, you need to articulate the major "first choice" reasons why volunteers are a meaningful, positively-selected strategy for strengthening your service delivery. It's also important to staff morale to affirm that the board intends to maintain funding levels to hire or keep employees. Volunteers offer a complementary, not alternative, way to expand available services.

Think about the unique characteristics of volunteers. Despite the flowery language of hearts and hands, the difference between volunteers and employees is not caring, concern, or enthusiasm. Commitment to quality service is an individual trait regardless of a paycheck, and most nonprofit employees are dedicated workers. However, in general:

- Volunteers have perceived credibility with clients, donors, legislators and others for the very reason that volunteers do not gain financial profit from the organization.

- It often makes a difference to the recipient of service that the provider is there purely because he or she wants to be.

- Volunteers are more free to criticize and speak their minds.

- Volunteers bring the "luxury of focus" to their work. While the paid staff must spread their time and efforts equitably among all clients, volunteers can be recruited specifically to concentrate on selected individuals and projects.

---

2 For a complete discussion of why organizations involve volunteers, see *From the Top Down: The Executive Role in Volunteer Program Success*, revised edition, by Susan J. Ellis (Philadelphia: Energize, 1996).

- Volunteers, as private citizens, may be able to cut through red tape and bureaucracies more directly than employees, who are often limited by jurisdictional restrictions.

- Volunteers are usually different from (though not necessarily better or worse than) employees in terms of age, training, occupation and other factors. This lets volunteers offer "thinking outside the box."

- Volunteers can be asked to work odd hours, in different locations, and to fill special client needs for which staff time cannot be justified.

- Volunteers can experiment with new ideas and approaches that are not yet ready to be funded.

All of this is beyond the simple fact that volunteers bring the organization more hands, talents, and hours.

Vision

Volunteers are as diverse as the entire labor market. Stating that you want volunteers does not immediately translate into a clear picture of what that means. Your dreams set the direction for everyone to follow. Here are just a few questions to assist the board in articulating a vision for volunteer involvement:

- How do volunteers fit into our mission and goals? How do they connect to the way we want to be seen in the community?

- Ideally, what role or roles do we want volunteers to fill?

- What should our volunteers look and be like? Should they reflect or represent the clients/consumers we serve? Expand or augment the skills of our employees?

- What are the pros and cons of adapting our volunteer involvement to the emerging trends and issues in volunteerism (such as mandated community service by students, welfare-to-work plans, and corporate employee projects)? What criteria (political, ethical, financial) should we employ to determine which trends to pursue?

- How large should the volunteer program grow? At what point will we reconsider the financial and staff support we have allocated for this?

The vocabulary describing "volunteering" is in flux, encompassing such terms (and audiences) as: "community service," "service-learning," "pro bono projects," or "lay ministry." What your organization now calls its "volunteer program" may better be envisioned as a "community resource office."

Analyze possible outdated stereotypes you may have about the kind of person who volunteers. If you tend to consider volunteers as kindly older people or teenagers sent by their schools, it's clear that your vision of their contributions will be limited. By the law of self-fulfilling prophecy, if you expect the lowest common denominator, that's the program you'll create and that's what you'll get. Of course, the opposite also holds true. Aiming for the best and brightest people to volunteer in meaningful roles will result in a terrific talent pool. But you have to believe it first.

Planning

Has planning for volunteers been integrated into other planning for your organization? As with anything else, if you don't set goals, you may not accomplish anything – or you may end up doing the wrong things. Do you know what you want to achieve through volunteer action? Whom you want as volunteers in the coming years?

A common board activity today is "strategic planning." Are volunteers incorporated into your long-range plans for the organization? Or do you plan for everything else and then assume the unspoken "and volunteers will support all of this in some way"? It is possible and appropriate to take a proactive position on volunteer involvement: state what you want and then the staff can take the steps necessary to accomplish those goals. If you want a high-powered, expert, diverse volunteer corps – plan for it.

When the chief executive presents a new initiative, ask: "Have volunteers been considered in this plan?" For example, decisions about a merger affect volunteers in both settings just as they do both sets of employees. The design for a new building should include the space necessary to accommodate volunteer work, be it an activity area, storage space, or private work rooms.

In addition to planning *for* volunteers, solicit volunteers' input and ideas in any overall organization planning or evaluation process. Volunteers are familiar with the organization and committed to your success, but they are still community representatives. This gives them a unique perspective as "insider/outsiders." They may also have access to consumer/client opinions in a different way than employees do.

Risk Management

As with anyone who enters your doors, volunteers pose potential risk management questions and insurance needs. Volunteers are neither more nor less likely to have accidents or to do something wrong, but have you taken all the steps necessary to protect clients, volunteers and staff in the event an incident should occur?

Does your current insurance policy cover volunteers? If not, should you negotiate for this? Or will you provide individual excess liability coverage for some or all volunteers?

Are you willing to accept a degree of risk to gain the benefits of volunteer help? Or is fear of some worst-case scenario pushing you into risk "avoidance" rather than risk "management"? Lawyers and insurance agents should not be naysayers. If you truly want volunteer participation, search for safe and legal ways to facilitate it.

Policies

The following are areas in which it would be extremely helpful for the staff to have some policy guidance from the board:

- Which existing organization policies for employees apply to volunteers equally (example: confidentiality), which do not apply at all (example: sick leave), and which require adaptation (example: reimbursable training expenses)?

159

- What are the criteria for determining appropriate roles for volunteers and for determining that an activity is inappropriate for volunteers? If your employees are unionized, this policy area takes on even more importance. You may also need a policy for when and how volunteer issues are to be included in any contract negotiations with labor officials.

- What are our screening requirements for volunteers, such as police checks or child abuse history (which may cost money to obtain)? Are we comfortable with setting qualifications criteria for volunteers, even if this means turning some people away?

- What is our policy regarding discrimination against volunteer applicants, and do our public affirmative action statements include mention of volunteers?

- What are the bottom-line performance standards to which volunteers will be held accountable? Under what circumstances can a volunteer be fired?

- What are the principles for handling a dispute between an employee and a volunteer, or between a client and a volunteer?

- Will we reimburse volunteers for their out-of-pocket expenses? What criteria will we use to decide what other expenses, such as conference registration fees, we will or will not pay on behalf of volunteers?

As always, it is the role of staff to implement such policies. But the board can and should assure that such issues are being addressed.

Budget

It is axiomatic that "volunteers are not free labor." The board can demonstrate its understanding of this fact by assuring that funds are allocated for volunteer program needs. Here are some budget line items needed to support volunteers (other than staffing, which we'll discuss in a moment):

- Reimbursement for volunteer out-of-pocket expenses (often referred to as "enabling funds").

- Printing costs for recruitment materials, applications and other recordkeeping forms, training manuals and handouts, recognition certificates, etc.

- Expenses to cover orientation, training and continuing education for volunteers.

- Excess liability or auto insurance coverage.

- Supplies and equipment to allow volunteers to do their work. (To state the obvious, if you recruit volunteers to coach basketball, have you budgeted for basketballs?)

- Recognition costs, such as party refreshments and small tokens of appreciation.

All of this belongs on the organization's financial statements. The Financial Accounting Standards Board (FASB) nonprofit accounting guidelines now require the reporting of the value of some donated time, so it is legitimate to reflect the costs as well. Although many resist the notion as inappropriate to the spirit of volunteerism, it is indeed possible to establish a dollar value for the contribution of volunteers. Options range from using annually-calculated median values published by such sources as Independent Sector or the Points of Light Foundation, to a more accurate figure calculated specifically for your organization.[3] Reporting a dollar "balance sheet" for volunteer involvement transforms this hard-to-assess resource into a tangible asset. It also allows the board to see the true value, rather than simply the cost, of agency services.

Staffing

The chief executive is responsible for staffing the volunteer program, but the board should realize that the adequacy of staffing is a factor in the ability to achieve the vision and goals articulated by the board. Be willing to spend money on (and possibly raise

---

3 See the chapter on "The Dollar Value of Volunteers," by Alan S. Glazer, CPA, in *From the Top Down, ibid.*

money for) coordination of volunteers. If the executive proposes eliminating the director of volunteers position in times of a budget crunch, the board might ask whether this is shortsighted in terms of needing more volunteers in the future.

Evaluation

When was the last time anyone evaluated volunteer activity? Are volunteers doing the most needed things? Are they providing the best possible service to clients and staff? Is it actually costing more to have a volunteer program than it's worth? Are questions about volunteer accomplishments included in overall organizational self-assessment?

Employee resistance to volunteers is sometimes based on the observation that unpaid workers are not held accountable for their activities. Ineffective efforts (even counterproductive actions) are tolerated in the belief that bad public relations would result from criticizing or firing volunteers. When volunteers are also financial donors or have influential community connections, it is even harder for the paid staff to voice concerns. Does the board envision that volunteers will be expected to maintain as high a standard of work as employees?

Always remember that volunteers want to do the most good. Evaluation is therefore a form of recognition. It assures volunteers that their time and efforts are accomplishing something, and it implies that they have the capacity to learn and improve.

Outreach and Input

Volunteers expand the sphere of influence of the organization. Every volunteer is multiplied by dozens of relatives, neighbors, work colleagues, and others who have a source of firsthand information about your organization. Are these community members hearing (and repeating) gossip? Facts? Testimonials? Complaints? Volunteers influence potential consumers, donors, and voters. Your organization's goal is to make sure that influence is a good one.

Flipped around, volunteers are also a source of invaluable information because they offer the perspective of a community member not necessarily affected by a particular professional point of view. Their viewpoint is often substantively different from that of either the paid staff or the clients. Make sure, therefore, that volunteers are routinely surveyed as a part of any evaluation of your organization and that their point of view is reported and analyzed as a distinct factor. When applicable, consider the opinions of volunteers in reaching board decisions.

The direct-service volunteer corps is a source of people who can serve on board committees and perhaps become new board candidates. Why recruit board and committee members from a pool of strangers when it makes much more sense to invite those who are already informed about the organization? If you are concerned about confusing lines of authority, ask any volunteer chosen for the board to take a leave of absence from his or her direct-service volunteer assignment while serving on the board.

If the board cannot identify any direct-service volunteers with the skills to exercise leadership, perhaps the organization needs to reconsider its goals for volunteer assignments and recruitment. A well-managed volunteer program should bring in a wide range of people with a variety of talents and occupations. The board can express its interest in using the volunteer program as a training ground for prospective board members and then hold the organization's staff accountable for mobilizing such community members.

Volunteer Development as Resource Development

The goal of resource development is to obtain the support necessary to fulfill the organization's mission. Such support does not have to mean cash. Just as we acknowledge donated goods and in-kind services as alternative ways to achieve goals, strategically recruited volunteers can extend the budget. When a new project requiring funds is proposed, the board should ask: "What are all the ways we might try to support this new initiative, in addition to cash?"

Volunteers are never a substitute for adequate staffing. But one way to maximize the value of volunteers is to assign them "pioneer" roles – testing the feasibility of a new idea in a limited pilot project before going after full funding. Or a small corps of selected volunteers might assist one employee while the project gathers momentum. Volunteers with professional expertise might be asked for short-term technical assistance to make sure the project gets off the ground effectively. As trustees, board members have the role of assuring that every available resource has been considered before spending time and energy to raise more money. Volunteers are part of this resource mix.

Just as one cannot guarantee the success of a proposal-writing effort or a charity golf tournament, no one can promise that a campaign to recruit volunteers will elicit the perfect people with ideal schedules to offer. But does your organization devote as much attention to finding the right volunteers as it does to finding financial donors?

Recent surveys indicate that people who volunteer their time are also likely to donate money to causes they support – and that volunteers tend to give a higher percentage of their income to charity than do non-volunteers. Whether through board-led fund-raising or the efforts of the development staff, is your organization asking front-line volunteers to make a financial contribution as well? Is this a missed opportunity? Just make sure volunteers receive a completely different solicitation than uninvolved potential donors.

Conversely, are you missing the chance to mobilize donors as volunteers? Again, surveys show that when donors become involved firsthand, they often raise their financial contributions. So expand your resource development agenda to include inviting donors to become volunteers as well. This is especially effective if you are recruiting for one-day help, such as working at a special event. Treat donors as a talent pool, as well as check writers. You may, however, need a policy statement clarifying that just because someone is a donor, she or he is not automatically accepted as a volunteer. All volunteer applicants must be qualified and meet standards at the start of and during their commitment.

Self-led Volunteer Groups

The usual focus is on volunteers recruited to work within the organization, generally under the supervision of or in collaboration with paid staff. Another model for volunteer involvement is the independently-organized, self-governed volunteer group, organized specifically to benefit your organization. Whether called an auxiliary, friends group, or special event committee, such entities bring a whole new set of board considerations:

- Do we want a self-led volunteer group? Why, beyond hoping for increased fund-raising? Is this the best approach to achieving our goals?

- Are these to be independently-incorporated bodies, or will they use our organization's tax-exempt number and therefore require this board's oversight?

- How will such all-volunteer groups relate with the board, with the in-house volunteer department, and with one another?

- Who is in charge? Who "owns" the funds raised? Who approves name changes, project goals, and other public activities that affect our organization's community relations?

- Will our staff have any direct responsibility for or authority over any aspect of the volunteer group's work? Conversely, does the group have the right to delegate work to our employees?

- What reporting and evaluating will be done, and how?

- Should the president(s) of such groups serve on our board *ex officio*? If so, are their responsibilities the same as those of any other board member? What is the rationale for this group of volunteers being given governance privileges if direct-service volunteers (also contributors to our organization) do not?

You must balance the wish to allow supporters to be creative and active on your behalf with the obligation to exercise some control. If you already have an existing auxiliary or friends group, it is not too late to articulate the best working relationship. If you wish to explore the option of forming such a group, do so without dollar signs in your eyes. It takes time, effort, and nurturing to build a strong fund-raising corps. And how willing is the board to listen to input, as well as to accept checks?

Finally, you may want to create an advisory body or representational group, such as an alumni council. Be careful not to imply that these volunteers have decision-making authority. In fact, you should avoid calling the group an advisory "board" for this reason. The board of directors needs to clarify roles, lines of authority, and the conditions under which such volunteers will be consulted.

SUPPORT THE VOLUNTEER PROGRAM

Everything discussed so far is a tangible demonstration of board support for volunteer participation. As with any other activity, the time spent in thoughtful planning is repaid by an increase in accomplishments. If something is neglected, it may thrive by accident. But proactive support of volunteer involvement dramatically increases its potential achievement level. So what can a board of directors do to support a volunteer program after making the decisions above?

1. Regularly devote time to volunteers at board meetings.

This sends a strong message to everyone that volunteers are important. It will take time to discuss all the subjects already introduced. Once the volunteer program is under way, the board might periodically consider trends and issues having an impact on volunteer involvement, major goals for the coming year, and an overview of plans for recruitment, training, and recognition.

2. Analyze data about volunteer involvement.

Expect and discuss reports on the size and scope of volunteer activities, and integrate these into any assessment of organizational progress. Recognize that this is necessary to have a complete picture of the organization and of the resources available to it.

3. Participate in volunteer recruitment.

The more people spreading the word about volunteer opportunities, the better. Just as board members should be alert to fundraising potential, they should be on the lookout for ways to recruit volunteers. For example, each board member can:

- Recommend or refer candidates, with the understanding that they must go through the regular application process just as any other prospective volunteer.

- Distribute recruitment materials when doing public speaking on behalf of the organization or during visits to community sites.

- Arrange for the volunteer office to have access to your circle of contacts to share recruitment information, especially if you are employed by or affiliated with a corporation, religious institution, or other formal association. Identify company newsletters, special events or meetings, display booths, Internet listservs, or other ways to communicate with your colleagues. Be a visible advocate – explain why you chose to volunteer on the board of this particular organization.

- If possible, offer the volunteer office the expertise of your company's marketing or public relations staff and its graphic artists to design the best possible recruitment materials.

4. Take part in volunteer recognition events.

Attendance by the board shows other volunteers that they are valued at the top. Recognition events provide a great opportunity to mingle and talk with supporters of your organization, whose opinions may prove illuminating. Once at the event, contribute to its success with active participation, not observation from a segregated table. And, remember, *you* have also earned the thank-yous given to the organization's volunteers!

5. Make volunteers as visible as possible.

Include volunteer accomplishments in the organization's annual report. Incorporate information about volunteer opportunities into your organization's Web site for both recruitment of new volunteers and recognition of current ones. Make sure volunteers are included in any public forum or media outreach, and as agency representatives when appropriate.

6. Appoint a committee.

Some boards form a volunteer program advisory committee to offer ongoing advice, expertise, community contacts, and other resources to the volunteer program staff. In the absence of paid coordinating staff, you may want a board Volunteer Development Committee to plan the outreach strategies necessary to recruit the best volunteers. If yours is a membership association, volunteer-related issues may need to be considered by several committees, including the nominating committee and the membership development committee.

THE BOARD AS VOLUNTEERS

Board volunteers are at the top of the organizational chart and have specific legal and fiduciary responsibilities. They are perceived as very different from the front line, direct-service volunteers, who all too often are at the bottom of the chart. This dichotomy obscures important similarities between the two.

If you employ the best practices of effective volunteer management to working with board members, too, you'll notice a difference. This means writing complete position descriptions for board members, including all expectations, and then actively recruiting qualified people. It means requiring orientation and training, even if the new board member has status or influence outside the organization. You will also pay attention to interrelationships among board members, deal with volunteers who are not fulfilling their role, and enforce rotation policies. And you will thank people whenever they accomplish something (as well as at an annual event) and do everything necessary to help board members enjoy their service.

There may be ways to connect the in-house volunteer program with board work. For example, the volunteer office is continually welcoming new direct service volunteers. Can board members join one of those orientation sessions to learn about the organization, take the facility tour, and generally become acclimated? There will be additional information necessary for a board member to learn, but the basic orientation need not be duplicated.

While the line between governance and management should remain clear, it is hard to understand how the board can govern without any firsthand exposure to the work of the organization. As a part of ongoing board training, therefore, it is a great idea to ask every board member to fulfill a short-term (even if only a few hours) direct-service volunteer assignment once a year. Such "reality testing" may result in more appropriate governance decisions.

Recognize that even the most dedicated board member spends a limited number of hours pulled from a busy schedule on behalf of your organization. As with all other volunteers, when board members give of their time, they need to feel that time is valued, see that they are engaged in meaningful work, and enjoy their interactions with others. As a volunteer, don't you agree?

* * * *

One way to summarize this entire chapter is this: Too many organizations are thought*less* when it comes to volunteer involvement. The most important contribution you can make as a board member to maximize the value of volunteers is to become thought*ful* on the subject. Know why you want volunteers, consider the issues carefully, provide adequate resources, and successful strategies will follow.

Susan J. Ellis

When you first meet Susan Ellis, you are struck by her energy and intellect. It is also clear that volunteerism is not her job. It's her passion, which is why she has become an international expert on the subject.

Susan is President of Energize, Inc., an international training, consulting, and publishing firm that specializes in volunteerism. She founded the Philadelphia-based company in 1977 and since that time has assisted an amazingly diverse range of clients throughout North America, Latin America, and Europe to create or strengthen their volunteer corps.

She is the author or co-author of nine books, including *From the Top Down: The Executive Role in Volunteer Program Success, By the People: A History of Americans as Volunteers*, and *The Volunteer Recruitment Book*. From 1981 to 1987 she was Editor-in-Chief of *The Journal of Volunteer Administration*. She writes the national bi-monthly column, "On Volunteers," for *The NonProfit Times*.

Most recently, Susan has been exploring the potential of cyberspace for virtual volunteering and distance learning. The Energize Web site [www.energizeinc.com], created especially for leaders of volunteer efforts, is widely recognized as an innovative contribution to the volunteerism field. Susan is the volunteerism faculty member for the satellite broadcast series of the Learning Institute for Nonprofit Organizations (based in Madison, WI), in cooperation with the adult education division of PBS.

She has served on the national board of the Association for Volunteer Administration and the Internet Nonprofit Center, and is currently treasurer of the board of the New Society Educational Fund. She is an active volunteer in a variety of state, national, and international volunteerism associations.

Susan J. Ellis, President
Energize, Inc.
5450 Wissahickon Avenue, Philadelphia, PA 19144
voice: 215-438-8342 • fax: 215-438-0434
e-mail: susan@energizeinc.com
Web site: http://www.energizeinc.com

CHAPTER 10

Internet Strategies for Nonprofit Organizations

Steve Epner

Introduction

Becoming a part of the Internet can be a powerful tool for a nonprofit organization. It can help generate membership, spread information and even help with raising money.

Best of all, board members need not be computer experts to lead an organization into this arena. Just asking the right questions of other experts can help them make the many decisions that are involved.

Internet Overview

Everyone is talking about the Internet. It is everywhere. At home, school and business. Articles appear every day in some publication. It can be intimidating. It is confusing.

The Internet is like a spider web of giant pipes that carry information around the world. Inside the web, the pipes provide interconnections between physical locations. Each site may have thousands of users connected to it.

Originally, the Internet was designed by the military. Now average people have discovered its many uses. As more people wanted to be on the Internet, the problem of how to make it available to everyone who wanted a connection arose. Thus, the ISP, or Internet Service Provider, was born. An ISP buys a connection or link into the Internet and resells Internet connectivity to the public.

ISPs have grown and spread across the world. Some are basement operations run by a few "techno-nerds" (as we lovingly refer to them). Others are part of multinational giants such as AT&T, MCI, and Sprint. Then there are the ISPs that have grown up in the current environment. Some of the best-known are AOL, UUNet, and PSINet.

Some have grown too fast and cannot support all of their users. Others are unreliable with inadequate backup or security. Not all are well-managed or financially sound. It is a minefield out there, and you must be careful where you commit your operation. Add to this the fact that millions of new users are getting on the Internet every month, and it is easy to become overwhelmed.

Given this background, there is a fear that the Internet will experience brownouts or even a crash. AOL's well-publicized problems may be just the tip of an iceberg. The Internet was never designed to handle the traffic load that is being placed on it. Promoters are telling everyone not to worry, that the necessary infrastructure will be added as needed. Doomsayers are predicting that, as movies, telephone and other high-volume uses increase, the sheer weight will bring the Internet to its knees. The backlash, they say, would destroy the Internet for the near term. Who is right? No one knows. If you are going to get on the Internet, you have to be flexible.

On the Internet, everyone talks about finding, reading and surfing for "home pages." Very simply, a home page is the first information that is transmitted from a specific location. The amount of data has nothing to do with a page. It can be one line or hundreds of screens full of information.

Home pages are kept or "hosted" at Web sites that have large-capacity connections to the Internet. Each of these sites is operational twenty-four hours a day, seven days a week. There are special backups and other technology to make sure that the data is accessible whenever someone might come looking for it. If your ISP is down, you do not exist. This is one of the main reasons so many organizations (including Fortune 500 companies) have opted to rent space on large Web hosting sites, rather than to build and maintain their own.

Web hosts also take care of security, installing "fire walls" to protect information. These fire walls keep uninvited guests from tampering with the data and programs at the Web site. Security has become a key topic of survival. Every day, hackers come up with new ways to cause trouble. This is one of the scariest aspects of the Internet world today. For example, protecting your client and donor lists is a top priority. We have all dealt before with the question of whether to sell name lists. Now the choice is tougher. If you publicize your active names online, anyone can easily take them electronically. In an automated world, everything happens faster and sometimes in surprising ways.

Surfing may be the most publicized fun on the Internet, but one of the most important uses for the Internet is e-mail. E-mail is basically typed voice mail. Like voice mail, people assume it is being read (listened to) and acted upon. If you are not prepared to retrieve your e-mail regularly, do not start using it. It may become a negative for you and your correspondents.

E-mail is the foundation of many of the opportunities that are important to a nonprofit organization. This is a basic method of communication between people and organizations. It is cheap and easy. Because nonprofit organizations are traditionally underfunded and understaffed, it is always important to find ways to augment limited resources.

Anyone who wants to receive e-mail on the Internet must have an address. It consists of a name or identity, an @, and a service provider name. For example, sepner@thinknet.net is Steve Epner's mailbox located at the ISP called Thinknet.

The provider name is called a "domain" and is recognized by the Internet as a physical location where information can be sent. It is up to the domain to then sort and deliver e-mail to its subscribers. The proper term for this process is "store and forward."

An organization or individual may decide to buy its own domain name to have a fixed identity and an address that won't change if its ISP changes.

For example, my company (BSW Consulting, Inc.) owns the domain "bswc.com." Now my e-mail address is sepner@bswc.com. The domain can be moved to any ISP anywhere in the world and still be found. ISPs charge an extra fee to create a "virtual host" (your domain attached to their site), but it is worth the price.

Getting a domain is easy. You'll find all of the instructions at "www.internic.net" on the Internet. The work can be completed online, and you will be invoiced for the registration fee. The cost is $35 per year with two years paid upfront.

If the forms intimidate you, ask an Internet-savvy 16-year-old or a knowledgeable volunteer to help. If you can't find either, most ISPs will do the work for about $100. Or consider setting up a community service project to get help from local high schools or colleges.

Just do it now as most of the three- and four-letter acronyms are already registered. As a nonprofit, your name will most likely end in "dot O R G" or ".org" as it is typed. A number of organizations also reserve the same name under the "dot C O M" extension to make themselves easier to find.

AT&T, in a recent reference to the Internet said, "It is not about technology, it is a new dial tone." The implication is overwhelming. Anyone who has seen an 8-year-old on the Internet knows that young people are as comfortable online as the older generation is on the telephone. This is the way your future board members, staff, clients and donors will communicate.

Organizations and their members need to begin to experiment now. While the long-term picture is unclear, what is evident is that the critical mass is building. Americans online are mostly young, educated and in higher income brackets. These are the people you need to find. The next generation of workers will have grown up with computers and automation. Successful organizations must provide the tools this generation will demand if they are to attract and keep the best and the brightest.

Why Get on the Internet?

The most important strategic question is: "Why should we get on the Internet?" There are many reasons. Vanity motivates some groups – "We just have to have a presence because all of the other charities have one." So does competition – "If we don't do it, our donors may invest their discretionary dollars elsewhere."

In examining this question, it is important to first understand what activities fit the Internet. Below is an outline of information that an organization may choose to make available on the Internet, organized as it might appear on a home page.

The term "link" or "linked" is used to describe the ability to transfer to another area within or external to the Web site. Links make it easy to move around a site. They also reduce the amount of information that must be transmitted every time a visitor arrives.

Certain information on a Web site may need restricted access. For example, a strategic plan in development may not be released for public comment until the board of directors approves it. Along the same lines, financial reports may not be made public until the audit is complete. Having private or restricted areas will support the effective and efficient operation of the organization.

Outline of Internet Information

General Information

Welcome statement and overview

Mission / vision statement

Strategic plan

History of the group

Sponsored and related activities

Where to find information on the Web site

Bylaws

Officers, directors, staff

Contact information

Frequently asked questions (FAQ)

Client Participation Information

Benefits

Application forms

Referral information

Special education (with a description of each program and necessary forms)

> Lending library
>
> Sponsored programs
>
> University-sponsored programs with client discounts
>
> Interactive educational programs

Client-centered chat room (may be restricted to registered clients and advice only)

Volunteer Participation Information

Requirements for each position or opportunity

Application forms

Rosters

Stakeholders

Volunteers

Publications (current and archive issues/articles)

Newsletters

Magazines

Conference proceedings

Links to other appropriate publications

Operation (Parts may be restricted)

Committee areas (virtual meeting space and minutes)

Committee reports

Calendar of events

Event information

Financial Information (may be restricted)

Financial statements (includes Form 990)

Budgets

Audit report

Government Affairs

Fund-raising

Solicitations

Acceptance of gifts (tributes, designated gifts, special programs)

Merchandise sales

Notes on Internet Information

Organization General Information

One of the most important functions of a Web site should be to inform the public and to recruit new clients, donors and stakeholders. Anyone who arrives at the Web site should be able to gain a quick understanding of the group and its mission. Activities, history and a description of the full Web site need to be available.

This is the place to introduce your officers, directors, staff and volunteers. Pictures and biographical sketches are friendly ways to promote your most important players and to recognize them for their work.

While in this area, people unfamiliar with your organization should be able to find its mission or vision statements, strategic plans, and goals. You may even use the section to survey potential participants. Ask a few questions as part of registering their names. It is a good way to get feedback and leads for new talent.

Finally, contact information should be provided. This should include whom to contact, by area of responsibility, and ways to contact them. Phone, voice mail, e-mail, U.S. mail, and fax information need to be available. Include all regional or local offices and affiliates. Make it easy for people to get in touch with you once they have found your Internet site.

Client and Volunteer Participation Information

Here, the forms and benefits of participation should be presented in such a way as to entice prospective stakeholders, volunteers and others. Existing participants may find this area useful, too, as they often misplace the original literature they received, which explained the benefits of the organization.

Chat rooms are a recent addition to many nonprofit Web sites. Here, people can gather electronically to discuss common concerns. A chat room can be a general area for sharing ideas on operation, programs, or plans. Or it can be an online support group. Some of these programs can be sponsored and happen at fixed times. Or monitors or other professionals may assist the attendees in getting the most from the experience.

Application forms should be available. Real-time referrals for client-required services could be considered a major benefit.

Volunteers who sign up online can be put in immediate touch with like-minded people already involved with the group.

Rosters

In this section, rosters of clients or donors may be made available. Organizations differ on whether these lists should be kept confidential. Client lists are rarely posted on the Web. With donor lists, donors should have a say in whether they want to be listed.

Publications

There is a great deal of discussion on whether all publications of an organization should be available to the public. Some nonprofits treat their newsletters and magazines as a valuable benefit. Making them available to the public might lessen the incentive for some to participate as stakeholders. To resolve this question, many organizations have set up tiers of accessibility to their publications.

For example, current publications (and often those going back some number of issues) may be restricted to active subscribers only. Archived information is usually made available to the public. The information in the public archive is normally at least one issue behind what's current.

Operations

Committee Areas: The Internet provides the capability of establishing virtual meeting space for committees and other groups. The meeting areas (where work in process is kept) may be restricted to participants in the committee only. At a minimum, each committee should have its own area. It should include a listing of members, their e-mail addresses, a calendar of events, and meeting minutes.

Additional space can be provided for virtual committees or task forces to work on projects. For example, there may be a project to do strategic planning for the group. Each person could obtain the latest information, update it with comments and place it back out in the virtual meeting space for others to read.

In the future, it will be possible to have interactive meeting sites. These will include the ability to share "white board space" and other applications, such as spreadsheets. Technology vendors have already demonstrated the use of two-way videoconferences as part of this capability. In the meantime, chat rooms provide the ability to have an online meeting using typed communications in place of voice.

Committee Reports: This is an area where final reports from committees can be made available. A history of reports should be posted here as background for new members of the organization or of a committee.

Calendar of Events: Each nonprofit can publish a complete calendar of upcoming meetings, conferences, educational seminars, and other events. The calendar should extend into multiple years. Where possible, "links" to related information within the Web site should be provided.

Conference Information: When a conference is coming up, post a standard agenda of events, costs, transportation and registration details online. Participants should be able to complete and e-mail forms for attendance and lodging.

Financial Information: In this area, current and historical financial statements, budgets and audit reports may be made available. Most nonprofit organizations are required to regularly publish financial information. While printed copies of the IRS forms (990) are still necessary if requested, posting the information online may reduce these requests, as well as the time and costs associated with responding to them.

Benefits

Special Education: Lending libraries are often underutilized because people do not know what is available. Here is a place to brag about what can be obtained. The status of materials (checked out or on the shelf) and any waiting list may be viewed. An online order form should be provided, as well as a form to request that additional materials be added to the library.

Sponsored Programs: University programs and other types of education can be publicized here. Special interactive programs, built specifically for Internet distribution, will soon become available.

Sponsored Newsgroups: Newsgroups are an excellent way to create recognition for the organization. It is here that the stakeholders can discuss specific issues. Or those targeted for help from a charity can meet online. For example, people suffering from a specific disease could meet to discuss coping strategies.

A properly designed application for access to these areas will reduce concerns about liability. Consult your Web site designer or counsel for advice on what kind of liability disclaimer to post. The organization must be careful to not take on any responsibility or liability for the answers and other information that may be provided.

Government Affairs: General reports and copies of pending legislation may be included. If there are updates on specific bills, state regulations or related items, here is a fast, inexpensive way to quickly update the membership. Also, members may be encouraged to send e-mail to members of Congress to support special causes.

Fund-raising

Solicitations: E-mail and other electronic means offer an inexpensive way to ask for money. This can be part of a regular solicitation program or for special events. The use of electronic mail lets organizations maintain closer contact with members while reducing the overall cost of operations.

Related fund-raising programs can be instituted, such as the online monitoring of a program. For example, it would be possible to track the care and status of a "poster child."

Acceptance of Gifts (tributes, designated gifts, special programs): Gifts can now be accepted online 24 hours a day, 7 days a week. Someone who wants to make a donation in honor of an occasion can now enter the information using an interactive form. The information from this form can be used to automatically acknowledge receipt and to send an online or regular mail announcement to the person being honored.

Virtual Fund-raising: Programs such as silent auctions can be operated online as fund-raisers. These can be held at regular times or continuously throughout the year.

Strategic Issues

Organizations must consider many high-level, strategic issues when planning their Internet presence. Do not rely on what others have done. What works well for one group may not work at all for another.

The first, and one of the most important considerations for most nonprofits, will be revenue impact. Every company that will want to sell Web site services will promise the organization new sources of revenue. However, it is important to remember that donors are asked to spend money in many different ways. Be sure that any new inflow of cash related to one of the above Internet-related programs is not offset by a loss of revenue in other areas.

501(c)(3) status may be affected by some activities. Rules and regulations related to the effect of selling services or products through a Web site, the selling of Web space and other services are in flux. Questions related to income treatment and accounting are beyond the scope of this article. Competent legal and audit advice should be obtained.

Organizations that sponsor Newsgroups or other "chat" areas may be liable for invalid advice. Be extremely careful in developing, publicizing and supporting any type of interactive bulletin board that would create an "expert" environment. A disclaimer should be printed at the entrance to any such bulletin boards and inside the bulletin board as well. Many organizations will even require that a potential user read and agree to the limitations of liability before participating in the site. Think this area through carefully. The expert bulletin board may be one of the best things an organization can do to attract new members and potential donors for its charities.

There also may be some liability for the organization if it posts inaccurate information about a client, stakeholder or other parties. What if a volunteer posts something that is untrue? In some cases working their way through the courts, the Web site host is being held responsible for content it made available. As the host, a non-profit may have to review and approve everything that is posted.

This potential brings up another issue. How will the staff time necessary to manage the Web site be provided? Experience is indicating that groups need about one full-time-equivalent position to update their information monthly and maintain a quality Web site. Ask the question: What will not get done or where will the salary for another person come from?

Here is a perfect area to get volunteer labor. Many people have some expertise in creating and maintaining simple Web sites. These may be professionals on the board (or an individual who works for a member of the board), hobbyists or even teen-agers. Groups should also consider asking for assistance from graduate or undergraduate students who want experience or projects for school.

Part of the contract for an Internet site should include a provision for obtaining the demographic and address information of all visitors. This raises the questions of how data related to potential clients or volunteers might be distributed. Will the organization sell the list of visitors? If there is an extra charge for address information, how will it be paid?

After reviewing the above, many nonprofits may ask the strategic question: "Why do we want to do this?" Even with a large number of unknowns, there are many things that are positive about the use of the Internet and electronic communications.

One reason to be out there is to attract new clients, volunteers, and donors. From an operational point of view, the Internet offers a number of opportunities to reduce operational costs. For example, using the Internet as a way for committee members to confer will save travel and planning expenses if the number of in-person meetings can be reduced.

In general, e-mail is less expensive than long-distance telephone charges. It can also be a very efficient way to distribute material to members. Most Internet Service Providers do not base charges on the volume of material being sent. Internet broadcasting can replace broadcast fax due to lower cost, speed and ease of use.

Further, the progressive nonprofit will find ways to use the Internet to reduce other time-consuming operations. The list is limited only by the imagination.

Strategically, the Internet should allow greater communication with participants. There can be daily updates on issues critical to your stakeholders. Consider including research, government action or critical issues that could not be afforded any other way. Late-breaking stories or legislative alerts can be disseminated quickly without tying up a fax line to individually dial hundreds of phone numbers.

One last strategic warning: Many of the Internet capabilities are new to organizations. Because there is not a long history of programs to be observed, results cannot be accurately predicted. Manage the expectations of other board members and stakeholders carefully before undertaking any new programs.

Web Site Basics

Creating a presence on the Web involves more than just having a technician type some information on a computer. A well-done Web site will attract visitors who will return time after time. Good home pages contain valuable information that is updated regularly. Without updates, a site will be visited only once or twice.

There are five keys to a good Web site. The first is speed. Most Web surfers are of the MTV generation. They are impatient and want to get information now! Any site that takes more than thirty seconds before information can be read will be left. The best sites bring up text information quickly and only then start to download fancy images that take more time.

Second, the page must look good. A good graphic designer is a must for a truly professional-looking Web site. Make the site attractive, but simple. Fancy backgrounds, for example, often do not print well. This means that an interested prospect may not be able to print out a readable, black-and-white copy of the information from your site.

Next, the information must be interesting and substantive. Put more than fluff on the site. The organization will want to develop a reputation in the Web world that will have the effect of sending others to visit and learn from your site.

Fourth is the need for constant change. The most sought-after pages are updated daily. Most organizations and their participants can get by with monthly updates for general information and weekly updates for project-related reporting.

Finally, the best Web reputation anyone can achieve is to be the page of choice to get information on a specific subject. Once a quality site is set up, it must be heavily publicized. Make sure your prospects know where to find answers. Then help them. After a short while, yours will be the place to come for answers. When that happens, you will find new participants.

Once the Web site is in place, carefully consider adding Hot Links. These are jumping-off points that take surfers to related locations on the Web. Links can be very helpful, but be careful. You may lose control of the visitor or connect them with a site that leaves a bad impression. Always check out any Web site that will be a link from your own.

A good exercise for every nonprofit deciding to "get on the Net" is to define "what is success?" The definition should be based on measurable results. This can provide a basis for negotiating the actual fees necessary to make a site viable. Bonus dollars can be provided for demonstrable reductions in operating expenses. For example, if donors make payments electronically as a result of Web-based requests, the Web host can be given a bonus of some percentage of the payment.

Selecting an Internet Service Provider

After the decision is made to get on the Internet, it is important to find the right help to get there. Because the Internet is relatively new, few firms have long track records. Often the most innovative providers are the newest. Therefore, the selection and contracting are critical tasks.

The first decision is whether to do the work in-house. Managing technical people and coordinating efforts with artists are not part of normal board-member training. In most cases, the organization will be well-served to retain the proper expertise to do it right the first time. One option is to get it done with volunteers. Many nonprofit boards have contacts with many service providers. The incremental cost of providing Internet services is low, so a strong board connection may get your group free service.

In choosing vendors, a standard Request For Proposal (RFP) form can help in the selection process. The most important section of an RFP is that of dealing with the specific requirements of the nonprofit and its members. Be clear and accurate in every request so that each potential vendor will answer the same questions. Legal counsel should review the format. For information on how to get a Request for Proposal form, see the end of this chapter.

Once the RFP process begins, do not play favorites. As much as possible, treat each vendor the same. Make sure that each gets prompt answers to questions that may affect proposals. Hold off on demonstrations until a preliminary evaluation is complete.

When responses are received, they should be reviewed in detail. Begin with an evaluation of the benefits provided by the proposed solution. Few responses will be able to do one hundred percent of what was requested. Therefore, the goal is to identify which vendors can provide the greatest degree of high-priority benefits. Rank the proposals.

Second, evaluate the risks associated with each proposal. What if a key person leaves? Will there be sufficient capital for the firm to stay in business? Is the firm so busy that the organization's work will not be completed in a timely manner?

Again, rank the responses. One may offer more benefit but at a significantly higher risk.

The final element of the evaluation is cost. Cost should be divided into start-up and maintenance expenses. In getting started, the organization may have to purchase hardware and software license agreements to be fully operational. Then there may be charges associated with designing and building the Web site.

The ongoing costs may overwhelm the initial charges. A five-year projection should be done. With the fast pace of change, the numbers will probably be wrong, but they will provide a means of comparing the alternatives.

Once a "prime suspect" is selected, it is time to negotiate. A number of issues should be covered. The first is ownership of the information and site design. If the vendors own the work you have paid for, it can be costly to move even if the vendor does not follow through on any number of promises. We suggest that the nonprofit and its members own the code and designs used to create the Web site. (To comply with copyright laws, the nonprofit may need to buy some software.)

Next, request full domain names for the nonprofit and its members. Many of the Internet Service Providers use their domain and publish the site names under their identity. Again, as long as everyone is happy, it may not make a difference. However, if there is any problem that may cause a group to consider a change, having your own domain will make that easier and less costly.

Another benefit of individual domains is that prospects for the organization or its members can find you without having to go through someone else. If the organization does not have a personal domain, then every time the Web site is advertised, you are advertising the Internet Service Provider.

When cost is to be evaluated, there are many Web sites that can be checked for pricing. Actual charges for any aspect of using the Web change so quickly that long-term contracts may not be in the best interest of the users. Communication costs are dropping.

Competition for Web servicing is way up. The trend will be to reduce the cost to attract the most content. Take advantage of competition.

Make sure that charges for updates are also projected. Remember that a stale home page will not be revisited. Plan to create at least monthly updates. The organization may want an ability to have weekly changes.

Finally, be flexible. There are no rules on the Internet. Keep in touch with others who are getting services from various providers. Find out what has worked well and what has not. Learn from their mistakes.

The Request for Proposal

Copies of a standard Request for Proposal form are available at the BSW Consulting Web Site: www.bswc.com. Call BSW Consulting at (314) 991-8505 for additional information.

The RFP contains descriptions of its various sections in *italicized* type. Where a word is found between two ampersands, it is to be removed and replaced by an appropriate word. For example, &ORGANIZATION& is to be replaced with the formal name of the organization creating the RFP. An easy way to accomplish this is to use the "Find and Replace" command.

Organizations that do not have access to the Internet may call for a copy on diskette. There is a nominal charge to cover the cost of the diskette, postage and handling.

Steve Epner

All you have to do is look at Steve Epner's office to know who he is. Most offices have work stations. Steve has play stations. Amongst his piles of computer literature and pictures of his wife and sons, are magic tricks and toys of every description and type.

His fascination with all that surrounds him is what makes Steve a sought after consultant, speaker and author. He makes technology simple and the simple magical.

Steve's early background includes experience in every phase of corporate information systems. Beginning as an operator in a "tab shop" environment in 1966, Steve has progressed through the various roles involved in operations, programming, system development, project management, and general management. As a consultant, Steve helps businesses to more effectively utilize their information resources. As president of BSW Consulting, Inc., he has established an enviable reputation for working with clients to develop business plans that do not end up collecting dust on a shelf and for finding ways to use information as a competitive tool. Advisory services are available to companies of various sizes in many different vertical markets. Mr. Epner understands that technology is valuable only if it solves real business problems. He encourages active involvement from all levels of management and staff. Steve works with project teams to take ownership, diagnose situations, focus on high priority issues, discover unique solutions and manage for success.

Steve facilitates strategic and tactical planning meetings for organizations of all kinds. He is an expert at encouraging competing views to be expressed without allowing the meeting to degenerate into a shouting match. Many sessions include training the client organization to manage future meetings. As an author and speaker, Mr. Epner has addressed both technical and nontechnical groups. He appears at conferences, shows, and meetings across the country. Over four hundred articles have appeared in major industry, technical and business journals.

Steve is the founder (1976) and past president of the Independent Computer Consultants Association. ICCA recently honored Steve at their twentieth anniversary celebration. Steve continues to be active in leading the consulting industry toward goals of professionalism and responsibility to the client community. Steve is the immediate past president of the St. Louis Gateway Chapter of the National Speakers Association.

Steve Epner
BSW Consulting, Inc.
1050 N. Lindbergh Blvd.
St. Louis, MO 63132
314-991-8505
Fax: 314-432-3130
E-mail: advise@bswc.com
www.bswc.com